SPRING 2019

JAN 1 THESS - PHIL
FEB HEB & JAMES
MAR 1 PET - JUDE
APR REVELATION

OnTrack Devotions: Spring 2019

Published by:
Pilgrimage Educational Resources
1362 Fords Pond Road, Clarks Summit, PA 18411
www.simplyapilgrim.com

For subscription information:
Pilgrimage Educational Resources
1362 Fords Pond Road, Clarks Summit, PA 18411
570.504.1463
ontrackdevotions.com

Printed in the United States of America

Copyright © 2018 Pilgrimage Educational Resources

All rights reserved. No part of this publication may be reproduced, stored in a retrieval system, or transmitted in any form or by any means - for example, electronic, photocopy, recording - without the prior written permission of the publisher. The only exception is brief quotations in printed reviews.

Any internet addresses, email addresses, phone numbers, and physical addresses in this book are accurate at the time of publication. They are provided as a resource. Pilgrimage Educational Resources does not endorse them or vouch for their content or permanence.

Author: Dwight E. Peterson
Executive Developer: Benjamin J. Wilhite
Editor: Kristin N. Jones

ISBN-13 978-0-9600241-0-0
ISBN-10 0-9600241-0-7
10 9 8 7 6 5 4 3 2 1

QUICK START GUIDE

Everyone is at a different place in their walk with God and in their Bible study skill. Because of that, OnTrack is designed to engage four progressive user **SKILL LEVELS**. This guide will help you identify your skill level and how to use OnTrack effectively.

IDENTIFY YOUR PERSONAL SKILL LEVEL

Be honest about your own personal level as you begin! Starting beyond your actual level can lead to unnecessary frustration and discouragement. Some level of frustration is good when learning a skill, but too much may tempt you to give up. Pay particular attention to the approach each user should take based on their current **SKILL LEVEL**.

Level 1: You have spent little or no time in personal Bible study and you have limited knowledge of the Bible. **FOCUS: Key Passage, Devotional Thought.**

Level 2: Most of your experience with the Bible is from church and/or at home. You have been taught from the Bible, but you have not consistently studied it on your own. **FOCUS: Extra Reading, Devotional Thought, answer at least the first two Daily Questions if you can.**

Level 3: You have a bit of experience reading the Bible on your own. Maybe it hasn't always been consistent or you are newer at it, but you are getting comfortable with it. **FOCUS: Extra Reading, Devotional Thought, answer all four Daily Questions.**

Level 4: You have a lot of experience in Bible study and you consistently see solid applications. **Focus: Extra Reading, Devotional Thought, all Daily Questions, and try creating your own questions.**

Every once in awhile, review your current skill level to check whether you should bump it up. You can do this on your own, with an accountability partner, or with a spiritual mentor. Aim to grow!

HOW TO USE ONTRACK

This tool is designed to help you grow your personal Bible study skill as a key part of developing a regular personal conversation with God. You will learn to dig into the text with good questions that lead to understanding and personal life change. To get the most out of OnTrack, follow the progression below:

PRAY. Ask the Holy Spirit to show you exactly what He wants you to see and understand from the Word. If you are in Christ, the Holy Spirit is in you and one of His jobs is to illuminate Scripture for you. He was the person of the Godhead directly engaged in the inspiration of the Word and He knows exactly what He meant when He wrote it.

READ THE WORD. Always start with reading the passage first before reading the devotional thought or any other tools you use to help understand Scripture.

QUICK START GUIDE, CONTINUED

What God has to say is always more important than what anyone else has to say about what God has to say.

READ THE DEVOTIONAL THOUGHT. The purpose of this text is to frame your thinking and to spur good questions, not to tie the passage up with a neat tidy bow.

ANSWER THE QUESTIONS. Some days, the author provides specific questions for you to answer that will help you dig into the text a bit. Other days, you'll see the generic Observation, Interpretation, Application, and Implementation questions. These are days designed to stretch you in the process of creating your own good questions.

ENGAGE OTHERS. One of the key benefits of a tool like OnTrack is that others in your world are working through the same Bible passages every day and engaging the same questions. This provides accountability for you; but more than that, it gives you an opportunity to compare notes and learn with each other. Often, you will see things they did not and vice versa. Bible study can be a team sport! It will help deepen your understanding of Scripture and your relationships.

GET ORIENTED

The following is a quick orientation to a typical OTD day. Use the sample devotional day image on the opposite page for reference.

1. **Header Bar:** It gives you the day of the week, the date, the theme, and the key passage for the day. Read the passage in your Bible BEFORE jumping to the next step!
2. **Extra Reading:** This is the complete text for the day. The key passage from the header bar will be in there, but this covers the context of the passage. If you are ready to bite off the whole chunk of Scripture, go for it!
3. **Devotional Thought:** The daily thought is designed to frame your thinking process AFTER you read the verses and BEFORE you answer the questions. It will encourage you to chew on the verses and ponder what God is telling you through His Word. The thought models for you the method of Bible study you are learning for yourself.
4. **Questions:** Each day will have four questions that help you personally work through the process of identifying what God is saying in His Word, then connecting it to your own life. Each question builds on the one before it.

A FINAL NOTE

Be patient and consistent. It's a process. Go at a comfortable pace. Ask God to grow your skill and to give you the discipline to keep at it. It will take time, but if you stick with it, you will be able to study God's Word for yourself.

#ontrackdevos

01.12.19 | SATURDAY

1 TIMOTHY 1:12-17

SO THAT

SAY WHAT?
Observation: What do I see?

SO WHAT?
Interpretation: What does it mean?

NOW WHAT?
Application: How does it apply to me?

THEN WHAT?
Implementation: What do I do?

How do you feel when you think about what it means to be saved? Too often, people seem to be apathetic about their salvation, especially those saved as children. It is almost as if it all seems to be fairly routine to them. What they sometimes miss is the incredible reality of what happened and why it happened. Paul had never gotten over the fact that Jesus Christ had saved him. He stressed that, in spite of his behavior and past, God had, by His grace, changed his life. In verse 16, he explained why God had saved him. It was so his life would be an example to others of what Jesus Christ could do. Even though he was once a "violent man," he was changed by Christ. His own salvation gave hope to other violent men. What difference has believing in Jesus Christ made in your life? How is your life different from those who do not know Christ? Is there someone you know who needs to see and hear the ways in which Christ changed your life? Your life is an example of what God can do. Can the unsaved see it? Circle the words "so that in me" in your Bible to remind you of your mission. Then ask God to use you.

EXTRA READING
1 TIMOTHY 1

ontrackdevotions.com

All Scripture is breathed out by God and profitable for **teaching**, for **reproof**, for **correction**, and for **training in righteousness**, that the man of God may be complete, equipped for every good work.

2 Tim. 3:16-17 (ESV)

ontrackdevotions.com

 @ontrackdevos

 facebook.com/ontrackdevos

JANUARY
2019
1 THESSALONIANS-
PHILEMON

MONTHLY PRAYER SHEET

"...The prayer of a righteous man is powerful and effective." James 5:16

Reach out...	How I will do it...	How it went...

Other requests...	Answered	How it was answered...

MONTHLY COMMITMENT SHEET

Name: _____

This sheet is designed to help you make personal commitments each month that will help you grow in your walk with God. Fill it out by determining
1. What will push you
2. What you think you can achieve

If you need help filling out your commitments, seek out someone you trust who can help you. Share your commitments with those who will help keep you accountable to your personal commitment.

Personal Devotions:
How did I do with my commitment last month? _____
I will commit to read the OnTrack Bible passage and devotional thought _____ day(s) each week this month.

Church Attendance:
How did I do last month with my attendance? _____
I will attend Youth/Growth Group _____ time(s) this month.
I will attend the Sunday AM service _____ time(s) this month.
I will attend the Sunday PM service _____ time(s) this month.
I will attend _____ time(s) this month.
I will attend _____ time(s) this month.

Scripture Memory:
How did I do with Scripture memory last month? _____
I will memorize _____ key verse(s) from the daily OnTrack Devotions this month.

Outreach:
How did I do last month with sharing Christ? _____
I will share Christ with _____ person/people this month.
I will serve my local church this month by _____

Other Activities:
List any other opportunities such as events, prayer group, etc., that you will participate in this month. _____

ontrackdevotions.com

TUESDAY | 01.01.19
CONTINUALLY
1 THESSALONIANS 1:1-3

How often in a week do you pray? When you do pray, how much time do you spend talking with God? If we were going to describe your prayer life, what words would we use? As you have been reading through the New Testament these past few months, have you noticed how much time Paul spent in prayer talking with God? In today's reading, we see another example of Paul's prayer life. Paul wrote to this church that he prayed for them continually. He told them in his letter that he did not just mention them in prayer when he thanked God for his food, or when he prayed in public at a worship service. He prayed for them all the time. Could you say the same thing to anyone? Is there anything you are praying about continually? Do you spend enough time in prayer each day? Why not begin this new year by making a plan that grows your prayer life? Don't settle for having a "meal time only" kind of prayer life. As you begin to faithfully pray, you will see the amount of time increasing and God answering your prayers. If you need help creating a plan to improve your prayer life, ask someone who can help you. It will change your life and the lives of those you pray for.

SAY WHAT?
Observation: What do I see?

SO WHAT?
Interpretation: What does it mean?

NOW WHAT?
Application: How does it apply to me?

THEN WHAT?
Implementation: What do I do?

EXTRA READING
1 THESSALONIANS 1

01.02.19 | WEDNESDAY

1 THESSALONIANS 2:1-6

MOTIVATION

SAY WHAT?
Observation: What do I see?

SO WHAT?
Interpretation: What does it mean?

NOW WHAT?
Application: How does it apply to me?

THEN WHAT?
Implementation: What do I do?

Why didn't Paul give up when faced with great opposition and criticism? What was it that kept him going through it all? Although he had faced suffering, insults, and "strong opposition" in Phillipi, Paul tells us that they continued to share the gospel. Most would have given up, or at least toned it down to avoid some of the opposition, but Paul kept right on going. Why? The answer begins in verse 3. It was because their efforts were not based on error or wrong motives. They were not motivated by trying to win the approval of men or appearing to be spiritual. They shared because they were men who had been "entrusted" with the gospel. They could not keep such valuable information to themselves, no matter what sharing it might cost them. To them, they had no choice but to keep on sharing the gospel. How well do you stand up to opposition at school or work? Do you realize you have been entrusted with the greatest message on earth? Is your only motivation to please God? If you answered yes to both of these questions, then you will be a person who can stand against opposition.

EXTRA READING
1 THESSALONIANS 2

ontrackdevotions.com

THURSDAY | 01.03.19
CARING FOR PEOPLE
1 THESSALONIANS 3:1-8

How concerned are you about the people in your world? How concerned are you about how your friends are doing spiritually? Paul gave us an example in this passage of the kind of concern we should have for others. How do you measure up to it? He told this church that he had longed to see them and find out how they were doing. When he found himself unable to go personally, he sent Timothy. He couldn't endure not knowing what was going on in their lives. When he received a good report about their well being, he was comforted even though he personally was being persecuted and in great distress. His burden was lifted and his reaction was "now we really live because you are standing firm...." That is remarkable concern! Do people you know affect you in this way? Are you so concerned with their walk with God that you are constantly thinking of them? Do you wonder if they are faithfully having devotions? Do you wonder if they are overcoming temptation? Does their spiritual walk encourage your heart in the midst of your own troubles? If not, what can you do to begin to care for people like Paul demonstrates in today's reading?

SAY WHAT?
Observation: What do I see?

SO WHAT?
Interpretation: What does it mean?

NOW WHAT?
Application: How does it apply to me?

THEN WHAT?
Implementation: What do I do?

EXTRA READING
1 THESSALONIANS 3

01.04.19 | FRIDAY
1 THESSALONIANS 4:1-8
SEXUAL PURITY

SAY WHAT?
What verses in the Bible can you quote when you are tempted to have sex outside of marriage?

SO WHAT?
Make a list of Biblical characters and people you know whose lives were impacted by violating God's commands in this area.

NOW WHAT?
What specific plan can you create to ensure you remain sexually pure? Who can help you?

THEN WHAT?
What personal commitment should you make in light of this passage?

Why is it wrong to have sex outside of marriage? If someone asked you that question, what would you tell him? Could you take him to a specific passage in the Bible? Sadly, many Christians know what the Bible specifically says in this area, but do not know where, or are not able to give specific Biblical answers. Instead we give answers like it causes diseases or unwanted pregnancies. While those are legitimate reasons, they are not the reason a Christian should say no to sex outside of marriage. We should not have sex outside of marriage because God's Word tells us it is wrong. In this passage, Paul writes that we must avoid sexual immorality and learn to control our bodies. He further says to avoid it because, in God's eyes, it "wrongs" and "takes advantage" of the other person. We are to be sexually pure because God has called us to live holy lives, not because we fear STDs or pregnancy. This passage tells us that if we fail in this area, we are rejecting God. Sex outside of marriage is wrong because God's Word says it is sin. Underline verses 7 & 8 to remind yourself of this truth.

EXTRA READING
1 THESSALONIANS 4

ontrackdevotions.com

SATURDAY | 01.05.19
GRIEF
1 THESSALONIANS 4:13-18

Should we as Christians cry and become distraught over the death of a loved one? Some might use a passage like today's reading to support a position that Christians should not grieve when people die. A closer look at this section reveals that interpretation to be wrong. In reality, while Paul did say not to grieve when someone we love dies, he added an important clause, "like those who have no hope." We grieve, but not like those in the world who are without Christ. We know that someday we will be reunited with those we love who have trusted Christ by faith. For the unsaved, death means separation forever, not temporarily. There is no hope in death for them, and their sorrow reflects their lack of hope. While we sorrow at death because separation is painful, it is for a short time. Our sorrow needs to reflect the hope we have that one day we will be reunited with those who have died in Christ. So, when death comes, it's okay as a Christian to feel the grief and sorrow that it brings, but not like the unsaved who have no hope. Ask God to help you reflect your hope when someone you care about dies.

SAY WHAT?
Observation: What do I see?

SO WHAT?
Interpretation: What does it mean?

NOW WHAT?
Application: How does it apply to me?

THEN WHAT?
Implementation: What do I do?

EXTRA READING
1 THESSALONIANS 4

01.06.19 | SUNDAY

PROVERBS 22

The book of Proverbs was designed to help us in "attaining wisdom and discipline; in understanding words of insight; in acquiring a disciplined and prudent life, doing what is right and just and fair; in giving prudence to the simple, knowledge and discretion to the young." As you read through this chapter, write down the verses that are most significant to you in your present circumstances.

VERSE | WHAT TRUTH IT COMMUNICATES | HOW IT IMPACTS MY LIFE

ontrackdevotions.com

MONDAY | 01.07.19
RESPONSE TO PASTORS
1 THESSALONIANS 5:12-15

To whom was Paul referring in verses 12-13? Who was it that had worked hard among you and was over you "in the Lord?" As we read, it becomes clear that he was referring to pastors. Paul wanted this church to be sure they responded properly to those who worked hard on their behalf spiritually. What is the response that Paul wanted them to have? They should treat them with respect and hold them in highest regard in love. Pastors are special people who do a special job. God wants to make sure people in the church treat them correctly. How do you treat your pastor? Do you pray for and respect your youth pastor and the other pastors in your church? Do you hold them in high regard, always assuming the best of them? Do you support and encourage them by letting them know how much you appreciate their labor of love among you? When was the last time you told them how much you appreciated their efforts on your behalf? Why not do that today? You can do that not only by writing a simple note of thanks but, more importantly, by living a consistent, godly life. After all, this is what they have devoted their lives to help you do. Their reward is your faithfulness.

SAY WHAT?
Observation: What do I see?

SO WHAT?
Interpretation: What does it mean?

NOW WHAT?
Application: How does it apply to me?

THEN WHAT?
Implementation: What do I do?

EXTRA READING
1 THESSALONIANS 5

01.08.19 | TUESDAY
2 THESSALONIANS 1:1-4
TRIALS

SAY WHAT?
What trials or persecution have you endured in your life?

SO WHAT?
What positive qualities have they produced?

NOW WHAT?
What plan can you create to respond better when trials or persecution come into your life?

THEN WHAT?
What personal commitment can you make in light of this passage?

Can you think of positive results in people's lives due to trials or persecution? What positive characteristics are a part of your life because of the trials or persecution you have faced? Paul saw great characteristics in the church of the Thessalonians resulting from the trials they had undergone. He thanked God that, first of all, they had grown in their faith. Trials had helped them to trust God more and, as a result, they had grown to depend on Him in every area of their lives. Secondly, he thanked God that their trials produced in them a greater love for each other. It must have been exciting to be part of a church in which faith in God and love for others was continually growing. Perseverance produces many positive benefits in our lives, as well as in the lives of others. Realizing perseverance only comes through trials ought to affect our view of them. How do you view your present trial or difficulties? Don't complain about the difficulties you are facing. Allow God to use them to grow you. Use today's questions to get started.

EXTRA READING
2 THESSALONIANS 1

ontrackdevotions.com

WEDNESDAY | 01.09.19
REJECTION
2 THESSALONIANS 2:1-12

Why do people go to hell? Is God the one who chooses for some to spend eternity there? According to this passage, Paul confirms to the Thessalonians that people go to hell because they have refused to love the truth and to accept salvation. He lets them know that they have had the opportunity to hear and understand the message but have refused to love and believe it. An individual makes his own decision concerning his eternal destination. God doesn't do that for him. Even more sobering is the next statement. In verse 11, Paul tells us that after someone rejects salvation often enough, Satan is there to deceive him. He will believe the lie and, as a result, never be saved. It is a very serious decision to reject God's offer of salvation. Have you put it off or refused it? Could you be on your way to hell because of the choice you have made? Have you ever, by faith, trusted Christ for your salvation? Rejecting God over and over after hearing and understanding the gospel has disastrous consequences. Who do you know that needs to hear what this passage teaches?

SAY WHAT?
Observation: What do I see?

SO WHAT?
Interpretation: What does it mean?

NOW WHAT?
Application: How does it apply to me?

THEN WHAT?
Implementation: What do I do?

EXTRA READING
2 THESSALONIANS 2

01.10.19 | THURSDAY
2 THESSALONIANS 2:13-17
CHOSEN

SAY WHAT?
Observation: What do I see?

SO WHAT?
Interpretation: What does it mean?

NOW WHAT?
Application: How does it apply to me?

THEN WHAT?
Implementation: What do I do?

We read yesterday that a person goes to hell because he has chosen to reject the truth and refused salvation. Does that mean that those who are saved will go to heaven because they have chosen to accept the truth? The answer to that question is no, which can cause confusion about how salvation works in our lives. According to these verses, we go to heaven because God has chosen us. He called us to the Gospel. The Holy Spirit sanctified us so that we might share in the glory of Christ. It was not because of anything we had or could have done, but because of what God did that we are saved. This may not appear to make sense, but it is what the Bible teaches. People go to hell because of the choice they make. People go to heaven because of the choice God makes. While it may seem unfair, it is what the Bible teaches. If there is anything unfair about it, it is not that people go to hell (we all deserve that), but that some get to go to heaven. Knowing that God has chosen to extend grace to you should cause you to desire to serve Him with gratitude all the days of your life. Does it?

EXTRA READING
2 THESSALONIANS 2

ontrackdevotions.com

FRIDAY | 01.11.19
WORK ETHIC
2 THESSALONIANS 3:6-15

What does the word idle mean in this passage? How do we respond to idle people? The word translated in the NIV as "idle" is a military term which means "out of rank." It is a Christian who is acting "out of rank." In other words, it is a Christian who is not acting as he should. In this context, the specific behavior Paul had in mind was not working for a living or being lazy. What should our response be to a brother who is idle or being lazy? Paul tells us to keep away from him. That does not mean to withdraw with an air of superiority, but to be aloof, which demonstrates to him that we do not condone his work ethic. Paul explains that we should do this so that he feels ashamed. As we do, it will encourage him to do what is right. We must keep in mind that he is a brother in Christ and not our enemy. The goal is to demonstrate love and concern so that he will be won back to righteous living. We must always remember that our work ethic matters to God--so much so that we are to take a harsh view of those who do not work hard. How do you think God views the way you work? Are you setting the right kind of example?

SAY WHAT?
List the different places you demonstrate your work ethic.

SO WHAT?
How would people describe your work ethic in those places? Why?

NOW WHAT?
How can you become an even harder worker?

THEN WHAT?
What commitment can you make in light of this passage?

EXTRA READING
2 THESSALONIANS 3

01.12.19 | SATURDAY

1 TIMOTHY 1:12-17

SO THAT

SAY WHAT?
Observation: What do I see?

SO WHAT?
Interpretation: What does it mean?

NOW WHAT?
Application: How does it apply to me?

THEN WHAT?
Implementation: What do I do?

How do you feel when you think about what it means to be saved? Too often, people seem to be apathetic about their salvation, especially those saved as children. It is almost as if it all seems to be fairly routine to them. What they sometimes miss is the incredible reality of what happened and why it happened. Paul had never gotten over the fact that Jesus Christ had saved him. He stressed that, in spite of his behavior and past, God had, by His grace, changed his life. In verse 16, he explained why God had saved him. It was so his life would be an example to others of what Jesus Christ could do. Even though he was once a "violent man," he was changed by Christ. His own salvation gave hope to other violent men. What difference has believing in Jesus Christ made in your life? How is your life different from those who do not know Christ? Is there someone you know who needs to see and hear the ways in which Christ changed your life? Your life is an example of what God can do. Can the unsaved see it? Circle the words "so that in me" in your Bible to remind you of your mission. Then ask God to use you.

EXTRA READING
1 TIMOTHY 1

ontrackdevotions.com

SUNDAY | 01.13.19

PROVERBS 23

The book of Proverbs was designed to help us in "attaining wisdom and discipline; in understanding words of insight; in acquiring a disciplined and prudent life, doing what is right and just and fair; in giving prudence to the simple, knowledge and discretion to the young." As you read through this chapter, write down the verses that are most significant to you in your present circumstances.

VERSE	WHAT TRUTH IT COMMUNICATES	HOW IT IMPACTS MY LIFE

01.14.19 | MONDAY
1 TIMOTHY 2:8-15 — MODESTY

SAY WHAT?
If asked, what words would people use to describe you?

SO WHAT?
What words would you want them to use?

NOW WHAT?
How can you ensure that people notice you for your service to God and not your physical appearance or accomplishments?

THEN WHAT?
What personal commitment should you make in light of this passage?

Do you think Paul is saying it is wrong for women to wear jewelry or braid their hair? There are some people who think that is what Paul is saying. A closer look at this chapter, however, clearly shows that those who think that he is teaching against jewelry or braided hair are missing his point. The principle Paul wanted us to grasp is modesty. Modesty, in this context, does not simply have to do with not dressing sensually, but also includes dressing so that you do not bring attention to your physical appearance. He uses these examples to illustrate the types of dress that can bring attention to your body if you are not careful. Instead, according to verse 10, women should be noticed for their good deeds. His point was that women should not be known or noticed for how they look, but for the kind of people they are. What are you noticed for? When people talk about you, what do they say? For a girl who wants to please God, her priority should not be her looks, but her service to God and others. It may not be what the world tells you, but it is what God wants, which is all that really matters.

EXTRA READING
1 TIMOTHY 2

ontrackdevotions.com

TUESDAY | 01.15.19
QUALIFICATIONS
1 TIMOTHY 3:8-16

In today's reading, Paul lists for Timothy some important requirements for anyone who wants to be a pastor or deacon. It includes requirements for pastors, verses 1-7, and deacons, verses 8-10 and verses 12-13. He even gives requirements for the wives of these men in verse 11. It is a standard that not many people are able to meet. Why is this kind of standard so important? The answer is found in verse 15. The local church is the body of Christ and the pillar and foundation of the truth. It is the means God has chosen to take the gospel to the world. There is simply too much at stake to allow unqualified people to hold the positions of deacon or pastor in our churches. Before holding a leadership position, we need to understand these requirements and be accountable among ourselves to meet the requirements given in this section of Scripture. If you feel God may be leading you to be a pastor or deacon, it's important to begin working towards meeting these qualifications and be certain that anyone you choose to marry meets them as well. Our churches ministries are too significant for us to not have qualified people in leadership.

SAY WHAT?
Observation: What do I see?

SO WHAT?
Interpretation: What does it mean?

NOW WHAT?
Application: How does it apply to me?

THEN WHAT?
Implementation: What do I do?

EXTRA READING
1 TIMOTHY 3

01.16.19 | WEDNESDAY
1 TIMOTHY 4:6-16
AN EXAMPLE

SAY WHAT?
How would you rate yourself in the five areas mentioned?

SO WHAT?
In what ways have you allowed or not allowed people to look down on you in those five areas?

NOW WHAT?
In what ways can you change in order to be an example in these areas?

THEN WHAT?
What personal commitment can you make in light of this passage?

How much difference can a student make in this world? Do you have to be an adult to be able to really touch the lives of people? How old do you need to be before people are impacted by your life? Paul gave Timothy an important command in today's reading that answers those questions. It is found in a verse that would be great for you to memorize. Paul told Timothy, in verse 12, to not allow people to look down on him because he was young. In other words, do not give people a reason to look down on you or make you feel unimportant or insignificant in terms of your ability to impact your world. Instead, you should strive to be an example. You should set the example in your speech, conduct, love, faith, and purity. Maybe the reason so few teens positively influence others is that they do not set an example for people in these areas. How would you rate yourself in these five areas? If you are going to influence others, you have to be someone they respect. You have to be an example in your speech, your life, your conduct, your love, your faith and your purity. Are you?

EXTRA READING
1 TIMOTHY 4

ontrackdevotions.com

THURSDAY | 01.17.19
WIDOWS

1 TIMOTHY 5:1-16

In today's reading, Paul gives Timothy some specific instructions on taking care of the widows in the church. It is obvious from this passage that the care of widows is very important to God. The job of the church is to determine which widows are really in need and should then be put on a list to be cared for by the church, and which ones should not be put on the list. According to this passage, the first responsibility to care for a widow falls to her children and/or grandchildren. The men of her family are the first to assume the responsibility and, if there are no sons or grandsons, her daughters should care for her. God views it as repayment for the care the mother once gave to her children. The church then cares for widows who have no family or whose family is not fulfilling its Biblical responsibility. God views the care of widows so highly that He says if a man does not care for his widowed mother or grandmother, he has denied the faith and is worse than an unbeliever. The responsibility to eventually care for our parents or grandparents is clearly ours. Make the commitment that you will fulfill that future responsibility towards your parents one day, if it becomes necessary.

SAY WHAT?
Observation: What do I see?

SO WHAT?
Interpretation: What does it mean?

NOW WHAT?
Application: How does it apply to me?

THEN WHAT?
Implementation: What do I do?

EXTRA READING
1 TIMOTHY 5

01.18.19 | FRIDAY
1 TIMOTHY 5:17-25 — DOUBLE HONOR

SAY WHAT?
Observation: What do I see?

SO WHAT?
Interpretation: What does it mean?

NOW WHAT?
Application: How does it apply to me?

THEN WHAT?
Implementation: What do I do?

How are the pastors of your church treated? Do they get the respect and concern that they deserve? Paul let Timothy know that a pastor deserves special treatment in two specific areas. It is important for us to know what they are so that we do our part to see that they are followed in our churches. First, Paul wrote that a pastor who is leading his church well is worthy of "double honor." That is, he is worthy of double pay or a double salary, especially if his job is preaching and teaching. In a typical church, it is often communicated that a pastor should receive less because he is in the ministry. That is not what God's Word says. Secondly, he is to be protected from accusations against him. In fact, unless it comes from two or three witnesses, we should never consider an accusation. That means we cannot even entertain the idea that it might be true. On the other hand, if he is found to be in sin, he is to be rebuked publicly so that others will take warning. While the pastorate is a position of honor and should be viewed as such, it is also a position of great responsibility. How do you view your pastors? In what way can you encourage them today?

EXTRA READING
1 TIMOTHY 5

ontrackdevotions.com

SATURDAY | 01.19.19
MATERIALISM
1 TIMOTHY 6:3-10

What is your goal in life? How will you determine what career you choose? There are some important principles in today's reading that you need to keep in mind when considering these questions. Did you notice what they are? Paul wanted Timothy to be sure to warn his people, as their pastor, concerning the dangers of materialism. People who make gaining wealth their priority are walking down a dangerous path. In fact, they will end up in ruin and destruction. Paul says that people who want to get rich fall into temptations, traps, and foolish and harmful desires. Those desires will ultimately lead them into ruin and destruction. Why? Because the love of money is a root of all kinds of evil. To choose money as your priority is to choose to destroy your life! God's way is to learn that godliness with contentment is "great" gain! Pursuing money leads to destruction and pursuing God leads to great gain. It is devastating to pursue something you think will give you what you want, only to find out it ruins your life. Make godliness your priority, not gaining money. Demonstrate it by the choices you make for your future!

SAY WHAT?
What are some of your goals in life?

SO WHAT?
How can you tell if materialism is part of your goals?

NOW WHAT?
How can you combat the love of money?

THEN WHAT?
What personal commitment can you make in light of this passage?

EXTRA READING
1 TIMOTHY 6

01.20.19 | SUNDAY

PROVERBS 24

The book of Proverbs was designed to help us in "attaining wisdom and discipline; in understanding words of insight; in acquiring a disciplined and prudent life, doing what is right and just and fair; in giving prudence to the simple, knowledge and discretion to the young." As you read through this chapter, write down the verses that are most significant to you in your present circumstances.

VERSE	WHAT TRUTH IT COMMUNICATES	HOW IT IMPACTS MY LIFE

ontrackdevotions.com

MONDAY | 01.21.19
GODLINESS
1 TIMOTHY 6:11-16

Did you notice the contrast between verses 11-16 and verses 9-10. In verses 9-10, we see a person who has made his goal the gaining of wealth. This person has made it the priority of his life. However, in verses 11-16, we see a person who has made obtaining godliness his goal. Paul follows up his instructions to Timothy about money with a discussion about what he ought to pursue instead. Paul tells Timothy to flee from the love of money and instead pursue six things. Number them in your Bible. The decisions you make should be determined by your goal to be more godly and not to make more money. Many Christians work in order to make money to buy a car or some other wanted item and do not pursue godliness at all. What an empty life that kind of pursuit brings. In reality, your priority will be either godliness or money. If we examine your life and the choices you are making, what would we conclude about your priorities? How do you demonstrate that you are pursuing the qualities Paul lists in verse 11? What needs to change to have your priorities reflect a pursuit of godliness?

SAY WHAT?
Observation: What do I see?

SO WHAT?
Interpretation: What does it mean?

NOW WHAT?
Application: How does it apply to me?

THEN WHAT?
Implementation: What do I do?

EXTRA READING
1 TIMOTHY 6

01.22.19 | TUESDAY

2 TIMOTHY 1:8-18

BRINGING JOY

SAY WHAT?
List the people who have contributed spiritually to your life.

SO WHAT?
In what ways does your life encourage or discourage them?

NOW WHAT?
What can you do to continue or begin to encourage them?

THEN WHAT?
What personal commitment should you make in light of this passage?

In what way does your life affect others? When a person remembers you or thinks of you, what comes to his mind? It surely must have encouraged Timothy's heart to know that he had positively influenced the life of the Apostle Paul. When Paul wrote this letter to Timothy, his life was difficult, and he already had endured much. He was in chains for his faith and, according to verse 15, had dear friends desert him. He must have been extremely discouraged at times. It would be likely that Paul had invested significant time in the lives of those who deserted him. Their rejection must have broken his heart. Timothy was different. Whenever Paul stopped to think of Timothy, he was filled with joy because of Timothy's faith. In the midst of great discouragement, Timothy brought Paul joy. Is your life such that those who think about you are filled with joy because of your walk with God? Or, do you bring them sorrow and cause for concern because of the choices you are making? We need to strive to live the kind of life that encourages those who are close to us and love us. What traits in your life bring joy to those who love you? What needs to change?

EXTRA READING
2 TIMOTHY 1

ontrackdevotions.com

WEDNESDAY | 01.23.19
FAITHFUL
2 TIMOTHY 2:8-13

Of all the statements in verses 11-13, which one does not follow the pattern of the others? Why is this question even important? Of the four statements given, only one has nothing to do with how we respond or act. In the first one, we learn that if we die with Christ, which means dying to ourselves and receiving Jesus Christ by faith, we will live. If we endure, then we will reign with Him. If we, however, disown Christ, then He will disown us. But what happens if we are faithless? Had Paul followed the same pattern as in the previous statements, he would have written, "If we are faithless, God will not be faithful." However, he changed the pattern and said that when we have no faith, when we doubt and do not trust, God will still be faithful. His faithfulness to us has nothing to do with the extent of our faithfulness to Him. Does it bring you joy to know that even when you have no faith, God is still faithful to you? Isn't it amazing to know that the difficult times that sometimes foster doubt and lack of confidence in God's provision don't affect His faithfulness to us? What a great God we serve!

SAY WHAT?
Observation: What do I see?

SO WHAT?
Interpretation: What does it mean?

NOW WHAT?
Application: How does it apply to me?

THEN WHAT?
Implementation: What do I do?

EXTRA READING
2 TIMOTHY 2

01.24.19 | THURSDAY

2 TIMOTHY 2:22-26

FLEEING

SAY WHAT?
What are some of the evil desires Paul might have had in mind when he wrote this to Timothy?

SO WHAT?
How can you better "flee" them?

NOW WHAT?
Give examples of some specific situations you might face in which you would need to apply this principle.

THEN WHAT?
What personal commitment can you make after reading these verses?

In today's reading, we find one of the most important principles in Scripture. Did you see it? It is found in verse 22. Paul wrote to Timothy that he needed to "flee the evil desires of youth." That is a command that literally means to stay as far away from sin and temptation as he could. There is no provision here to see how far one can go without actually sinning or try to discover how spiritually strong one is. He is to flee, run away from, anything that might encourage him to sin. It is not about where the line of sin is, but how far away from the line I can get. Too often, we allow ourselves to be in situations where we do not flee evil desires. In fact, we put ourselves in situations that encourage them. We watch TV programs or go places that don't motivate us to run from evil desires. We must concentrate our efforts on staying as far away as possible from evil desires and thoughts. How should this verse affect your week? As you make plans remember to flee evil desires. It is not about when you cross the line, but how far away from it you can get. Has that been your mindset lately? It should be.

EXTRA READING
2 TIMOTHY 2

ontrackdevotions.com

FRIDAY | 01.25.19
BIBLE READING — 2 TIMOTHY 3:10-17

How important to you is reading your Bible every day? Do you plan your day around your Bible reading, or do you "fit it in?" According to today's reading, it should be the most important thing you can do each day. It should be the one activity you determine never to miss. Paul reminds Timothy that the Bible has been inspired by God. Therefore, it is God's message to us. It contains no errors and provides absolutely everything we need. It is profitable for teaching, rebuking, correcting, and training in righteousness. Because it is God-inspired, it is naturally profitable in all those areas. We need no other outside source. In fact, it is what causes the man of God to become "thoroughly" equipped for "every" good work. If Timothy committed himself to study and know it, then the Bible would cause him to become a man who was equipped to do anything well. Can you think of anything you do in the course of a day that can accomplish this for you? How can you guarantee that Bible study will be the most important priority of your day? How can you ignore the Bible when it provides every answer to every issue that comes up in life?

SAY WHAT?
Observation: What do I see?

SO WHAT?
Interpretation: What does it mean?

NOW WHAT?
Application: How does it apply to me?

THEN WHAT?
Implementation: What do I do?

EXTRA READING
2 TIMOTHY 3

01.26.19 | SATURDAY

2 TIMOTHY 4:1-8

BE PREPARED

SAY WHAT?
What spiritual questions would you be prepared to answer?

SO WHAT?
What spiritual questions would you not be prepared to answer?

NOW WHAT?
What plan can you create to be prepared to answer those questions?

THEN WHAT?
What personal commitment should you make in light of this passage?

Would you be ready if someone came up to you today and asked you how to become a Christian? What if someone came up to you and asked how to gain victory over a temptation he was facing? Would you be ready to give him an answer? In today's reading, Paul gave Timothy an important charge, one we should all strive to achieve. He wrote, in verse 2, for Timothy to be ready both in season and out of season to give people answers for the hope Timothy had. Most of us would be ready in season, when we are expecting questions. But Timothy needed to also be ready out of season, when he faced the unexpected. In order to be ready out of season, he would have to make studying the Scriptures his priority and assume that he would need to have answers off the top of his head. What would it take for you to be ready to share your faith with someone? A daily study to prepare yourself for the opportunities God may bring into your life would be a good goal. You never know when your opportunity will come. If God gives you an opportunity, make sure you are ready!

EXTRA READING
2 TIMOTHY 4

ontrackdevotions.com

SUNDAY | 01.27.19

PROVERBS 25

The book of Proverbs was designed to help us in "attaining wisdom and discipline; in understanding words of insight; in acquiring a disciplined and prudent life, doing what is right and just and fair; in giving prudence to the simple, knowledge and discretion to the young." As you read through this chapter, write down the verses that are most significant to you in your present circumstances.

VERSE	WHAT TRUTH IT COMMUNICATES	HOW IT IMPACTS MY LIFE

01.28.19 | MONDAY
TITUS 1:1-9
PASTORS' KIDS

SAY WHAT?
Observation: What do I see?

SO WHAT?
Interpretation: What does it mean?

NOW WHAT?
Application: How does it apply to me?

THEN WHAT?
Implementation: What do I do?

When searching for a pastor, what should a church look for? What qualities ought to be evident in his life? Paul answers that question in this passage. Paul gave Titus a crucial job. He was left by Paul in Crete to appoint elders, who were pastors, in every town. That is, of course, a huge responsibility. To be sure that he would appoint the right men, Paul left him specific instructions as to what qualifications these men should have in order to become a pastor. It is interesting that not only were there requirements for the pastor, but also requirements for his children. Paul told Titus to not only examine their personal lives, but also to examine the lives of their children. The children had to be believers, not disobedient or wild. Being a godly father is so important to being a pastor. If you are a pastor's child, your life can have an impact on whether your dad's ministry is a success or a failure. For those who are not children of pastors, the message for you is to pray for and encourage those who are, not criticize or judge. It is true that all children can help or hurt their parents' ministry. But for a pastor's child, it can also disqualify him from ministry.

EXTRA READING
TITUS 1

ontrackdevotions.com

TUESDAY | 01.29.19
SO THAT
TITUS 2:9-15

What do the words "so that" mean? Do they hold any significance for understanding this passage? These two words are significant in this chapter because they show Titus why Paul wanted him to teach specific things to certain groups of people. Titus taught certain truths to the older women "so that" no one would malign the word of God(vs5). He was to teach with integrity, seriousness, and soundness "so that" those who wanted to oppose him would have nothing to say(vs8). The third one ought to shake our apathy a bit. Titus taught the slaves truth "so that" the doctrines of God our Savior would be attractive. They probably had no idea the kind of impact they would have on people by just living the way Paul described. Their behavior could make the teaching about the Savior attractive. What impact does your behavior have on those who observe your life? Are the teachings about Jesus Christ attractive to them because of the way you live? What an awesome opportunity it is to influence those who see you! Why not circle "so that" each time it is used in your Bible, to remind you of why you need to obey.

SAY WHAT?
What kinds of behavior make the message of Jesus Christ attractive?

SO WHAT?
What kinds of behavior make the message of Jesus Christ unattractive?

NOW WHAT?
What can you do to make sure your behavior makes the teaching of Christ attractive?

THEN WHAT?
What personal commitment can you make in light of this passage?

EXTRA READING
TITUS 2

 #ontrackdevos

01.30.19 | WEDNESDAY
TITUS 3:1-8
OUR SALVATION

SAY WHAT?
Observation: What do I see?

SO WHAT?
Interpretation: What does it mean?

NOW WHAT?
Application: How does it apply to me?

THEN WHAT?
Implementation: What do I do?

Today we read one of the greatest descriptions of salvation in the Bible. It is a section we need to be familiar with whenever God gives us an opportunity to share our faith, or when we just need a simple reminder of what Jesus Christ has done in our lives. Paul begins, in verse 3, by describing what we were like before we trusted Christ. It is not very flattering, is it? In verses 4-6, he reminds us how we have been saved. Our salvation is the work of God in our lives and not something we can do for ourselves. Then, in verse 7, we are given the "so that" which concludes this thought. This happened so that we might have the hope of eternal life. And what should our response be to such truth? It should be to devote ourselves to doing good (vs8). Paul stressed these truths to Titus so he could remind his churches how incredible their salvation was. It would also serve to motivate them to do good. When we stop and consider what Christ has done for us, how can we do anything less? Reread this section and ask yourself what good you are doing in response to what God has done for you. Make sure your understanding of your salvation impacts the way you live!

EXTRA READING
TITUS 3

ontrackdevotions.com

THURSDAY | 01.31.19
PRAYER REQUESTS
PHILEMON 1-7

Although the theme of this book is forgiveness, and it contains much concerning the steps of forgiveness, there is also an awesome truth included about prayer. Did you see it? Paul began this personal letter with tender words to someone he loved very much. The first thoughts on his page were a reminder to Philemon that he thanked God whenever he prayed for him. Why? Paul had heard about his faith in the Lord and his love for the saints. Then Paul wrote down what he asked God for when he prayed. He asked God to make him active in sharing his faith. He wanted God to enable Philemon to see the opportunities to share what Christ had done in his life. He wanted him to be active in building relationships with the unsaved, that they might come to know Christ. What would happen in your youth group or church if you began to pray this prayer for each other? Think of the influence your church could have in your town if you were "active" in sharing your faith and building relationships with the unsaved. Why not choose three people to pray this for today. Write their names down and faithfully begin praying. Watch what God does!

SAY WHAT?
Who are the people you can pray this for today?

SO WHAT?
What might the impact be in their lives?

NOW WHAT?
What plan can you create to remain faithful in praying these things for them?

THEN WHAT?
What personal commitment should you make in light of this passage?

EXTRA READING
PHILEMON

ANCHOR
CHRISTIAN UNIVERSITY

THIS HOPE WE HAVE AS AN ANCHOR OF THE SOUL, A HOPE BOTH SURE AND STEADFAST AND ONE WHICH ENTERS WITHIN THE VEIL, WHERE JESUS HAS ENTERED AS A FORERUNNER FOR US...

HEBREWS 6:19-20

AMPLIFYING THE MISSION OF THE LOCAL CHURCH WORLDWIDE THROUGH FAITH-INFUSED BIBLICAL TRAINING AND EDUCATION.

DEGREE PROGRAMS:

CHRISTIAN LEADERSHIP FAMILY MINISTRY
CAMP MINISTRY URBAN MINISTRY
INTERCULTURAL MINISTRY YOUTH MINISTRY

ANCHORU.COM

We have this hope as an **ANCHOR** for the soul, firm and secure. It enters the inner sanctuary behind the curtain, where our forerunner, **JESUS**, has entered on our behalf.

Heb. 6:19-20a (NIV)

ontrackdevotions.com

 @ontrackdevos

 facebook.com/ontrackdevos

FEBRUARY
2019
HEBREWS & JAMES

MONTHLY PRAYER SHEET

"...The prayer of a righteous man is powerful and effective." James 5:16

Reach out...	How I will do it...	How it went...

Other requests...	Answered	How it was answered...

MONTHLY COMMITMENT SHEET

Name: _____

This sheet is designed to help you make personal commitments each month that will help you grow in your walk with God. Fill it out by determining
1. What will push you
2. What you think you can achieve

If you need help filling out your commitments, seek out someone you trust who can help you. Share your commitments with those who will help keep you accountable to your personal commitment.

Personal Devotions:
How did I do with my commitment last month? _____
I will commit to read the OnTrack Bible passage and devotional thought _____ day(s) each week this month.

Church Attendance:
How did I do last month with my attendance? _____
I will attend Youth/Growth Group _____ time(s) this month.
I will attend the Sunday AM service _____ time(s) this month.
I will attend the Sunday PM service _____ time(s) this month.
I will attend _____ time(s) this month.
I will attend _____ time(s) this month.

Scripture Memory:
How did I do with Scripture memory last month? _____
I will memorize _____ key verse(s) from the daily OnTrack Devotions this month.

Outreach:
How did I do last month with sharing Christ? _____
I will share Christ with _____ person/people this month.
I will serve my local church this month by _____

Other Activities:
List any other opportunities such as events, prayer group, etc., that you will participate in this month. _____

ontrackdevotions.com

FRIDAY | 02.01.19
WHO IS JESUS?
HEBREWS 1:1-7

What if Jesus Christ were just a higher form of an angel and not really equal with God? Is it even important for us to be able to make this distinction clear? Does it matter if Jesus is God or not? If Jesus is just a higher angelic form and not fully God, then one of the most important actions He took would not have been possible. The writer of Hebrews demonstrates Jesus Christ is not an angel, but is far superior to the angels. He first reminds us that, in the Old Testament, God spoke to people directly. But in the New Testament, He chose to speak to man through Jesus. He tells us that Jesus is superior to the angels because He created the universe. He is the radiance of God's glory and the "exact" representation of God. Consequently, this means Jesus is exactly like God in every way because He is God. As a result, He provided justification for our sins, which would not have been possible if He were merely an angel. After He paid the price for our sin, He returned to heaven and now sits at the Father's right hand, a position no angel can occupy. Jesus Christ came to earth to pay the price for our sin. We must respond to Him as God and receive by faith the gift of eternal life He offers. Have you?

SAY WHAT?
Observation: What do I see?

SO WHAT?
Interpretation: What does it mean?

NOW WHAT?
Application: How does it apply to me?

THEN WHAT?
Implementation: What do I do?

EXTRA READING
HEBREWS 1

02.02.19 | SATURDAY

HEBREWS 2:5-18
WHO IS JESUS?... CONTIN-

SAY WHAT?
What temptations are you now facing?

SO WHAT?
In what ways are the areas you are tempted in similar to what Jesus faced?

NOW WHAT?
How did Jesus respond to His temptations?

THEN WHAT?
Write out a prayer asking Jesus to help you be successful in the areas of temptation that you face.

Yesterday we learned that Jesus Christ is God. But why did He have to become a man? Why is this important? In today's reading, we are given some key reasons. One of those is found in verses 9 & 17. Jesus Christ became a man so that He could die for the sins of all mankind. He paid the price for our sin so we do not have to pay it ourselves. Another reason is given in verse 14. Jesus Christ became a man to destroy Satan, who had the power of death, so we could be free from the fear of death. The third reason, verses 17-18, is key for daily living, but few seem to realize it is true. Jesus Christ became a man to become a merciful and faithful High Priest. He experienced the daily walk of a man and is able to respond to us out of personal knowledge of those experiences. Further, verse 18 tells us that since He was a man, He is able to help us when we are tempted because He faced the same temptations. Since Jesus became a man, He not only knows temptations, but is able to help us resist our temptations. Use the questions presented today to help you better apply this truth to your life. In what ways are the areas you are tempted in similar to what Jesus faced?

•

EXTRA READING
HEBREWS 2

ontrackdevotions.com

SUNDAY | 02.03.19

PROVERBS 26

The book of Proverbs was designed to help us in "attaining wisdom and discipline; in understanding words of insight; in acquiring a disciplined and prudent life, doing what is right and just and fair; in giving prudence to the simple, knowledge and discretion to the young." As you read through this chapter, write down the verses that are most significant to you in your present circumstances.

VERSE	WHAT TRUTH IT COMMUNICATES	HOW IT IMPACTS MY LIFE

HEBREWS 3:12-19

02.04.19 | MONDAY

ENCOURAGE DAILY

SAY WHAT?
Observation: What do I see?

SO WHAT?
Interpretation: What does it mean?

NOW WHAT?
Application: How does it apply to me?

THEN WHAT?
Implementation: What do I do?

Have you ever known someone who at one time in their life walked with God, but now is far from Him? Have you ever wondered how that happens? Ever wondered what we, as brothers and sisters in Christ, can do to help prevent it from happening? The answers to these questions are in today's reading. The author warns about the possibility of turning to unbelief. He tells us, in verse 12, that one turns away from God after he first has begun to develop a sinful, unbelieving heart. His point is that you do not go to sleep at night with a great walk with God and wake up the next morning in total rebellion. It's a process that begins with developing a sinful, unbelieving heart and ends with us turning away from God. How do we help each other avoid this? According to verse 13, it is by encouraging one another daily. When we see something in another's life that concerns us, we need to speak up. If we are watching out for each other daily, we won't be very far from God before someone seeks to encourage and help us. Do you encourage daily? When is the last time you encouraged someone in his walk with God? Isn't it time you began?

EXTRA READING
HEBREWS 3

ontrackdevotions.com

TUESDAY | 02.05.19

PERSONAL RESPONSE

HEBREWS 4:1-7

Why couldn't some of the people of Israel enter the Promised Land? The answer to that question is important and helpful to us in making sure we do not miss out on heaven the way some missed out on the Promised Land. According to verse 2, people were excluded from the Promised Land because, although they had heard the message, they did not combine it with faith. They believed it intellectually, but they never accepted it by faith, personally. As a result, instead of obeying what they had heard, they acted in disobedience. It was possible to have seen all the miracles, have actually heard God speak directly, and still miss what God had for them. They did not respond by faith to what they had heard and did not live in obedience to the message they received. The truth is, this happens all the time in Christian families. It happens to teens whose parents take them to church every time the doors are open. They hear the Word, but they do not take the next step of combining it with personal faith and personally living in obedience to what they have heard. Tragically, they miss heaven because they are like the children of Israel. Could you be one of those people? How sad to see it all and miss it!

SAY WHAT?
Observation: What do I see?

SO WHAT?
Interpretation: What does it mean?

NOW WHAT?
Application: How does it apply to me?

THEN WHAT?
Implementation: What do I do?

EXTRA READING
HEBREWS 4

02.06.19 | WEDNESDAY

HEBREWS 4:14-16

HELP!

SAY WHAT?
What specific temptations are you now facing?

SO WHAT?
How does it help to know that God is a sympathetic High Priest?

NOW WHAT?
How can you approach Him with confidence to find mercy and grace?

THEN WHAT?
What personal commitment can you make in light of today's passage?

Can Jesus Christ really understand what you are going through? Does He really know how you feel when faced with temptation? Since He is God, can He identify with us in our moment of crisis? In today's reading, we have what may be one of the most encouraging sections of Scripture. It shows us that the answer to those questions is a definite YES! We have, in Jesus Christ, someone who knows exactly what we face in this culture. Verse 15 tells us that He was tempted in every way like we are and He is, therefore, a sympathetic High Priest. He faced what we face every day. However, He went through it with one major difference--He did not sin. He knows not only what we are going through, He knows how to help us go through it successfully. How should we respond to such truth? Verse 16 tells us that, because all this is true, we should approach the throne of grace in prayer with confidence. Why? Because Jesus Christ alone understands what we face, and He knows how to help us be successful. It is there that we "receive mercy and find grace to help us in our time of need." What circumstance are you currently facing that you need to take to God in prayer? Remember that He is always ready to help!

EXTRA READING
HEBREWS 4

ontrackdevotions.com

THURSDAY | 02.07.19
DEVELOPING MATURITY
HEBREWS 5:11-6:3

This passage gives us a vital principle we must understand in order to be able to grow to maturity in our walk with God. Did you see it? The author confronted the Hebrews because they did not progress as quickly as they should have in their walk with God. He told them that by this time they ought to be teachers, but they were still like infants who needed milk. He also explained that if one is to grow, he needs to move away from milk and into solid food. Solid food is for those who have trained themselves to distinguish between good and evil. In this passage, we find that milk is not just the simple truth of Scripture. It is Scripture that we accept intellectually. Meat, on the other hand, is that which tells us how we ought to live, the teachings about righteousness. Maturity is the ability to take what we are learning and apply it to our lives so that we can distinguish between good and evil. If we are going to grow, we need to apply what we are learning to our daily lives. We do not grow simply because we are gaining knowledge, but we grow when we take that knowledge and apply it to our lives. Spiritual maturity is based on how we act, not on what we know! How mature are you?

SAY WHAT?
Observation: What do I see?

SO WHAT?
Interpretation: What does it mean?

NOW WHAT?
Application: How does it apply to me?

THEN WHAT?
Implementation: What do I do?

EXTRA READING
HEBREWS 5

02.08.19 | FRIDAY

HEBREWS 6:13-20

PROMISES

SAY WHAT?
Observation: What do I see?

SO WHAT?
Interpretation: What does it mean?

NOW WHAT?
Application: How does it apply to me?

THEN WHAT?
Implementation: What do I do?

How confident can we be in God's promises? Could you bank your life on them? Today's passage confirms the answer is yes. To help us with our confidence, let's look at what God did for Abraham to help him develop confidence. In Genesis 15, God had Abraham take animals, cut them in half and place each half on opposite sides creating an aisle one could walk through. Why? Because in Abraham's culture, when two people made a commitment to each other, they walked through halved animals together. It symbolized that the one who was responsible for breaking the promise should be cut in half. Abraham finished arranging the animal pieces, but God caused him to fall asleep. God passed between them alone. This illustrated that the fulfillment of the promises God made depended on Him alone, and Abraham had nothing to do with it. That same commitment is made to us. According to verse 18, if our hope is placed in God, we will be greatly encouraged. Why? Because the fulfillment of His promises depends on Him alone, not on us. How amazing to know that the promises of God cannot be broken! Do your actions demonstrate you believe that?

EXTRA READING
HEBREWS 6

ontrackdevotions.com

SATURDAY | 02.09.19
BETTER
HEBREWS 7:18-28

This chapter is an amazing piece of Scripture! Although it may seem complicated and difficult to understand, there is much here to motivate us. Let's take a closer look. The author portrays a superior office and a superior system. Jesus Christ, the High Priest, and the New Testament system are superior to the Old Testament high priests and the Mosaic Law system. Under the old system, a priest served only for a period of time. Jesus Christ is our Priest forever. The old system required that the priest offer sacrifices for sins. Jesus Christ is our sacrifice. The old system merely covered sin. Jesus Christ takes sin and washes it away. We have a High Priest who can save us completely. Since He will never die, this new system will not change and will live on forever. Jesus Christ is all we need, and He has become our Priest. He has given us access to God in a way that no other priest before Him could. Have you taken advantage of what Christ has done for you under this new system? Have you trusted Him as your Savior? Have you taken advantage of the direct access you now have to God? Do not allow yourself to live under the new system and not use all it provides for you. Who in your world needs to know what this passage teaches?

SAY WHAT?
What does it mean to have access to God?

SO WHAT?
How would your life be different if you were living under the old system?

NOW WHAT?
In what ways are you taking advantage of the "new" system?

THEN WHAT?
In light of this passage, what personal commitment should you make?

EXTRA READING
HEBREWS 7

02.10.19 | SUNDAY

PROVERBS 27

The book of Proverbs was designed to help us in "attaining wisdom and discipline; in understanding words of insight; in acquiring a disciplined and prudent life, doing what is right and just and fair; in giving prudence to the simple, knowledge and discretion to the young." As you read through this chapter, write down the verses that are most significant to you in your present circumstances.

VERSE | WHAT TRUTH IT COMMUNICATES | HOW IT IMPACTS MY LIFE

ontrackdevotions.com

MONDAY | 02.11.19
SAT DOWN
HEBREWS 8:1-6

Why did the author tell us that our High Priest "sat down" at the right hand of the throne? Is this significant to us? It is if you understand the Old Testament system of law. Under that law, a priest never sat down. In fact, there wasn't even a place in the tabernacle for the priest to sit down. His job was never finished because the sacrifices he made for the sins of people were not sufficient to cover all of their sins. When they sinned again, the priest had to offer sacrifices again. Jesus Christ is different. Do you remember what He said just before He died on the cross? "It is finished." The sacrifice for sin was paid. There was no need for any other sacrifice or payment for sin--not for any sin you have committed or will commit. Our High Priest, Jesus Christ, sat down because His work was finished. He sat down because everything that needed to be done to enable us to have our sins forgiven was completed on the cross. There is nothing you or I can or need to do beyond what Jesus Christ already did on the cross. How complete is our salvation! How should we serve the One who provided this for us? With hearts filled with gratitude, every minute of every day that He gives us. Is that how you are living your life?

SAY WHAT?
Observation: What do I see?

SO WHAT?
Interpretation: What does it mean?

NOW WHAT?
Application: How does it apply to me?

THEN WHAT?
Implementation: What do I do?

EXTRA READING
HEBREWS 8

02.12.19 | TUESDAY

HEBREWS 9:11-14

GUILT FREE

SAY WHAT?
Observation: What do I see?

SO WHAT?
Interpretation: What does it mean?

NOW WHAT?
Application: How does it apply to me?

THEN WHAT?
Implementation: What do I do?

Is it possible to live with a clear conscience? Is it possible, even after having done something horrible, to not feel guilty forever? Yes, if we understand what the New Testament system we are learning about has done for us! This is one of the greatest passages we can use to give hope to people in our world of what Jesus Christ can do in their lives. The author explains that the gifts and sacrifices under the Old Testament law were not able to "clear the conscience." Can you imagine that? When a sin had been committed and the blood of an animal applied, it did not clear the conscience of guilt. The sin was covered, but not taken away. But we can have our consciences cleared. We can live guilt free. Verse 14 tells us that because of what Jesus Christ did for us on the cross, His blood can "cleanse" our consciences, not just cover our sin. We can have the burden of a guilty conscience removed. If a heavy conscience is haunting you, Jesus Christ can wipe it clean--not just cover the sin, but take it away. Is there a sin you've confessed that still haunts you? Do you realize that God has cleansed you and washed your sin away? How can you apply this truth in your life today? Who can help?

EXTRA READING
HEBREWS 9

ontrackdevotions.com

WEDNESDAY | 02.13.19
FORGIVEN!
HEBREWS 10:11-18

How do you feel when you have done something wrong? How do you feel after you have come to realize you did wrong, seek forgiveness, and it has been granted? Imagine what it would be like to feel guilty forever, never able to make it right or to ever have the guilt cleared. In today's reading, we are given the amazing truth of what Jesus Christ has done for us. This chapter, like yesterday's, emphasizes that Jesus Christ paid the price for our sins once and for all. We are reminded again that in the Old Testament, the priest had to continually offer sacrifices for sin. However, our priest, Jesus Christ, made the final sacrifice and then "sat down" because it was finished. What does that mean for us who have trusted Christ? We are forgiven once for all. There is nothing else we need to do to take care of our sin. In fact, God says in verse 17, our sins will be remembered no more. They are not only forgiven, but set aside and not remembered. What an incredible truth! Why not underline verses 17 and 18 in your Bible to remind you of what happened to you when you accepted Jesus Christ. Don't allow guilt to plague you and hinder your walk with God! Ask God to give you the ability to live as one who has truly been set free!

SAY WHAT?
Observation: What do I see?

SO WHAT?
Interpretation: What does it mean?

NOW WHAT?
Application: How does it apply to me?

THEN WHAT?
Implementation: What do I do?

EXTRA READING
HEBREWS 10

02.14.19 | THURSDAY

HEBREWS 10:19-31

LET US

SAY WHAT?
Which one of those five do you need to work on the most? Why?

SO WHAT?
What will you need to do to begin working on it today?

NOW WHAT?
What kind of plan can you create to see it happen? Who can help you?

THEN WHAT?
What personal commitment can you make in light of this passage?

How should we respond to the kind of truth we read about yesterday? The passage we are reading today answers that question. It gives to us five challenges all beginning with the words "let us." Number them in your Bible. First, we are to draw near to God. We can do this by being faithful in our devotions and making sure we spend time every day with Him in prayer. Second, we are to hold unswervingly to the hope we have. God is faithful, so we should not doubt or lose our confidence. Though it may not appear as if He has control at times, He does. Third, we are to consider how we can spur one another on toward love and good deeds. That is, how can we challenge others to become more like Christ? Notice he uses the word "spur." Spurs are not very comfortable when applied. Sometimes doing this for each other may not be very comfortable for us or them. Fourth, we need to make church attendance a priority. Meeting together as a body is not optional. Finally, we are to encourage each other. We are to do things that boost others' spirits. We should pray for and encourage each other daily. In light of all God has done for us, what else would we do? Use the questions for today to help you begin.

EXTRA READING
HEBREWS 10

ontrackdevotions.com

FRIDAY | 02.15.19
SURE AND CERTAIN
HEBREWS 11:1-7

To help you to think through this chapter and the next, keep this outline in mind. Mark it in your Bible. First, we receive a definition of faith (11:1-2). Second, we see what people who have faith can do (11:3-40). Third, we realize what we need to do in order to become people of faith ourselves (12:1-3). Finally, we realize what God will do to help us (12:4-13). What exactly is faith? According to verse 1, faith is being sure and certain. Faith is not hoping that something will work out, or even confidence that it will. Faith is being sure and certain it will. Do those two words describe your faith? According to verse 6, faith is being sure that God rewards those who earnestly seek Him. What are we certain of? That God exists, even though we cannot see or touch Him. It is only when our faith becomes something that we are sure and certain of that we can expect to step out for God like the men and women in this chapter did. They could not have done it based on a "I hope so" kind of faith. Are you sure that God rewards those who diligently seek Him? Are you certain that God exists? Does your life show it? If not, start asking God to give you a heart of faith that is sure and certain.

SAY WHAT?
Observation: What do I see?

SO WHAT?
Interpretation: What does it mean?

NOW WHAT?
Application: How does it apply to me?

THEN WHAT?
Implementation: What do I do?

EXTRA READING
HEBREWS 11

HEBREWS 11:23-28

02.16.19 | SATURDAY

LOOKING AHEAD

SAY WHAT?
Observation: What do I see?

SO WHAT?
Interpretation: What does it mean?

NOW WHAT?
Application: How does it apply to me?

THEN WHAT?
Implementation: What do I do?

What is the most important thing in the world to you? Hopefully, it is the same thing that was important to Moses. He was able to enjoy everything the world has to offer and values. As the grandson to Pharaoh, he had fame. Many would have wanted to be with him and have him as a friend. He had money--all the wealth of Egypt. He could have bought anything he wanted. Yet those things were not important to him. Although the world could never understand, he chose to be mistreated rather than to experience the pleasures of sin. He thought it was better to suffer persecution for being a child of God than to have treasure. Would you do the same? Would you choose to be mistreated if you could be popular? Would you choose to be picked on for being a Christian if, instead, you could have as much money as you would want? If you were "sure" of what you hope for, and "certain" of what you cannot see, you would. Like Moses, you would be looking ahead to the reward you know that God has for those who diligently seek Him. You would be sure it is far better than anything the world could ever give. So, are you doing what Moses did? If not, what next step do you need to take?

EXTRA READING
HEBREWS 11

ontrackdevotions.com

SUNDAY | 02.17.19
IT IS POSSIBLE
HEBREWS 12:1-11

Who is the cloud of witnesses talked about in vs. 1, and how do they help us? The cloud of witnesses are the people listed in chapter 11. They encourage us by demonstrating that it is possible to live the life of faith and influence your world. They give us hope by showing us it can be done! How do we become people of faith? First, by throwing off everything that hinders. That includes those things that are not sin, but slow us down and entangle us in our walk with God. Secondly, we must get rid of any sin that is in our lives. We cannot tolerate any sin, large or small, and expect to become people of faith. Third, we need to run with perseverance, realizing this walk of faith is a long distance race. We need to keep at it. Fourth, we focus on Jesus Christ. He needs to be our priority and the only one we seek to please. This passage also tells us, in verse 4, that we can be encouraged knowing that, whenever we get off track, God will discipline us to get us back where we need to be. We must not fight against the discipline, but allow it to train us. You see, it is possible to become a person of faith. You do your part and be confident that God will do His.

SAY WHAT?
Of the four steps listed in this passage, which one do you think would be the most difficult to accomplish? Why?

SO WHAT?
What would it take for you to implement these steps?

NOW WHAT?
What kind of plan can you create and who can help you to make them a reality in your life?

THEN WHAT?
What personal commitment can you make in light of this passage?

EXTRA READING
HEBREWS 12

02.18.19 | MONDAY

HEBREWS 12:12-17 **SEE TO IT**

SAY WHAT?
Observation: What do I see?

SO WHAT?
Interpretation: What does it mean?

NOW WHAT?
Application: How does it apply to me?

THEN WHAT?
Implementation: What do I do?

How important is it for us to be involved in the lives of others? According to today's reading, it is very important. This passage is a call to be hard at work in three areas. First, we are to work hard to live in peace with all men. We are to do whatever we can to avoid being a part of division or conflict. Secondly, we are to work hard to be holy. We are to do our best to keep ourselves from sin and to be faithful in our walks with God. Thirdly, the author tells us that we are to work hard to "see to it" that no one is involved in the following four areas: missing the grace of God, allowing a bitter root to grow, practicing sexual immorality, or being godless like Esau of the Old Testament. You can't fulfill your responsibility to "see to it" if you sit on the sidelines worrying only about yourself and not getting involved in the lives of others. How active are you in the lives of other students in your youth group or church? Are they having their devotions? Are they avoiding sin? What are they struggling with? Do they have any bitterness in their hearts? What would it take for you to be able to answer those kinds of questions? Who might need your encouragement today? Circle the words "see to it" to remind you to be involved in people's lives!

EXTRA READING
HEBREWS 12

ontrackdevotions.com

TUESDAY | 02.19.19
CONTENTMENT
HEBREWS 13:1-6

What one thing would give you contentment if you had it? If you could have anything in the world that you wanted, what would make you the happiest? The author, in today's reading, says something related to this question. In verse 5, we are told to keep ourselves from the love of money and be content with what we have. Why shouldn't we seek money? Why should we be content with the amount of money we have or make? According to verse 5, it is because God has said, "Never will I leave you; never will I forsake you." Do you realize what you are being told? To be discontented with what you have is to say that having God is not enough and we need more than Him to be happy. The love of money and discontentment has a direct correlation to how important God is to an individual. Our lack of contentment demonstrates that God is not enough to cause us to be happy. We need Him plus friends. We need Him plus better looks. We need him plus..., you fill in the blank. We should be able to live without possessions and still be content knowing God is with us. Check your level of contentment. What does it tell you about how important God is to you?

SAY WHAT?
Observation: What do I see?

SO WHAT?
Interpretation: What does it mean?

NOW WHAT?
Application: How does it apply to me?

THEN WHAT?
Implementation: What do I do?

EXTRA READING
HEBREWS 13

JAMES 1:12-18

02.20.19 | WEDNESDAY

AVOIDING SIN

SAY WHAT?
Read the following verses and write down what they say about how to stop my evil desires from dragging me away and enticing me. Romans 12:1-2; 1 Corinthians 6:19-20; Matthew 26:41; Romans 6:1-14

SO WHAT?
Read the following verses and write down what they say about how to stop desires that have dragged me away and are enticing me. 1 Corinthians 10:13; 2 Peter 2:9; 2 Timothy 2:22; Hebrews 4:15

NOW WHAT?
Read the following verses and write down what they say about how to stop desires that have already enticed me and are ready to result in sin. Philippians 4:8; Romans 12:2; Ephesians 4:20-24

THEN WHAT?
What personal commitment should I make in light of this passage?

Is it possible for you to resist temptation? The answer is yes, and today's reading has some very helpful insights on how to do that. James tells us, in verse 12, that the person who perseveres under temptation and does not give in is happy. In fact, he tells us that there is a crown awaiting those who have successfully resisted temptation in their lives. He then goes on to describe the steps that temptation takes before it becomes sin. We need to make sure we stop it along the way so that it does not result in sin or death. First, it begins with an evil desire. Second, that evil desire drags us away. That means to be distracted or lured away from safety. We become curious and let down our guard. Third, we are enticed. We are now away from safety and ready to take the plunge. Those desires are conceived in our mind and are all we think about. At this point, sin is just around the corner. All we are waiting for is an opportunity to sin, and an opportunity will come. However, if we stop the temptation at any point, we can resist sinning. At what point in the process of temptation are you? What do you need to do to stop the progression, before it becomes sin? Use today's questions to help you.

EXTRA READING
JAMES 1

ontrackdevotions.com

THURSDAY | 02.21.19
MERELY LISTENING?

JAMES 1:19-25

What is the difference between a "listener" and a "doer?" It may not be what you think it is. James explains the difference in today's reading and admonishes us not to be a "listener." A listener is someone who, when he hears the Word of God, looks at it. The word James used here means stopping and actually seeing what is there. In fact, he says the listener looks closely enough to be able to see himself as he really is. The problem is that he then walks away and doesn't act upon what he sees. He is the person who goes to a camp or to church and hears a message that causes him to see himself as he really is but, when the service ends, walks away and forgets what he heard or read. A "doer" is someone who also hears, but his look is different from the "listener." He sees something from which he can't look away. What he has seen is so shocking and moving to him that he can't forget it. The result? He walks away determined to do something about it. He is so moved that he can't forget it and makes the necessary changes in his life. Which one are you? What are you working to change based on what you have recently "heard?" Don't walk away and forget what needs to change!

SAY WHAT?
Observation: What do I see?

SO WHAT?
Interpretation: What does it mean?

NOW WHAT?
Application: How does it apply to me?

THEN WHAT?
Implementation: What do I do?

EXTRA READING
JAMES 1

02.22.19 | FRIDAY

JAMES 2:8-13 **FAVORITISM**

SAY WHAT?
Observation: What do I see?

SO WHAT?
Interpretation: What does it mean?

NOW WHAT?
Application: How does it apply to me?

THEN WHAT?
Implementation: What do I do?

Why are you guilty of violating the whole law if you stumble in just one area? Doesn't that seem extreme? Not when you understand James' point. The example James uses is showing favoritism. It is wrong to treat people differently for any reason. No matter what one's race is, his social status, or his financial situation, God expects us to treat everyone the same. James then says, if we do show favoritism, we are judged as though we have violated the whole law (vs.10). It seems to be similar to being punished for staying out all night when you were only 5 minutes late. It would appear unfair. It seems that way until we read Matthew 22:37-40. In this section of Scripture, Jesus says that the entire law hangs on two commandments. One of these is to love your neighbor as yourself. You see, if we show favoritism, then we violate one of the foundations of the law. If we really loved our neighbors as ourselves, we would never show favoritism. What follows in verse 13 is even more sobering. Did you see it? James tells us that God will not be merciful to us if we show favoritism to others. If God were to treat you the way you treat others, what would it be like? Are there areas where you show favoritism? What needs to change?

EXTRA READING
JAMES 2

ontrackdevotions.com

SATURDAY | 02.23.19

TRUE FAITH

JAMES 2:14-26

James asks a very important question in verse 14--whether or not a person's faith, which is not demonstrated by his actions, can save him. In other words, if someone says he is saved, but he does not have behavior that seems to demonstrate it, is he really saved? As you read through this section, it becomes obvious that James' answer is no. He is telling us that it is possible to have a faith that does not save you. ==Faith that does not change behavior is as useless, according to James, as a person who does not meet the needs of people when he becomes aware of them.== Likewise, this kind of faith is also useless in meeting our need for salvation. According to James, it is just dead faith (vs. 17). Does just believing in your head and knowing factually that Jesus is God and that He died and rose again enough to get you to heaven? According to James, it isn't (vs. 18-19). If you have the kind of saving faith seen here, you will demonstrate it by the way you live. As you examine your behavior, what do your actions tell you about your faith? Do they tell you that your faith is true saving faith, or have you deceived yourself? Underline verse 26 in your Bible to remind you to examine your life in light of your actions.

SAY WHAT?
What evidences would you see in the life of someone who is genuinely saved?

SO WHAT?
What evidences do you see in your own life?

NOW WHAT?
What behavior could deceive someone into believing he is saved when he is not?

THEN WHAT?
In light of this passage, what personal commitment can you make?

EXTRA READING
JAMES 2

02.24.19 | SUNDAY
JAMES 3:1-12
OUR TONGUES

SAY WHAT?
Observation: What do I see?

SO WHAT?
Interpretation: What does it mean?

NOW WHAT?
Application: How does it apply to me?

THEN WHAT?
Implementation: What do I do?

What do you want to do in your future? Could God have full-time vocational ministry in your future? If you think God may be leading you into a ministry in which you would be teaching, today's reading should concern you. James tells us that teaching is not for everyone. In fact, those who teach will be judged by a stricter standard than others. That is a sobering standard when we think about the sin in our lives. What makes it even more serious is that teachers have to deal with their tongues and the danger they present just like everyone else. However, if you are going to be a teacher, you must realize that your tongue may be a small thing, but can cause great damage. Teachers must realize that the tongue can do irreparable damage. They must also realize that only through the power of God can it be tamed. If you are going to be a teacher, you must learn to control your tongue. If you don't, then you should pursue another vocation. Does the way you use your tongue allow you to be a teacher? Is your tongue being used by God to bring others to Christ, or used by Satan to hurt and discourage them? What can you do to better use your tongue and qualify yourself to be a teacher?

EXTRA READING
JAMES 3

ontrackdevotions.com

MONDAY | 02.25.19
WISDOM

JAMES 3:13-18

How can we tell if we are using God's wisdom or our own? According to today's reading, we simply need to look at the results in our lives from the choices we make. Knowing whether or not we have God's wisdom is very important. We read in chapter one that if we ask God for it, He will give it to us. But we also know that our selfish pride can often get in the way of using God's wisdom. We can easily allow our selfishness and pride to influence our decisions. James tells us that we can distinguish between those who are using godly wisdom or worldly wisdom by the results in their lives. Decisions made with worldly wisdom produce bitter envy, selfishness, disorder, and evil. We see an amazing contrast between those traits and the description of the results of godly wisdom. God's wisdom produces peace, consideration, sincerity, etc. James ends this chapter with a great promise. He tells us that those who seek God's wisdom and peace will reap a harvest of righteousness. What a great motivation to use God's wisdom and never our own worldly wisdom. As you examine the results of decisions in your life, whose wisdom are you using? Take a close look at your life. What characteristics do you see?

SAY WHAT?
How would the results of worldly wisdom be revealed in our lives?

SO WHAT?
How would the results of godly wisdom be revealed in our lives?

NOW WHAT?
What steps can you take to make sure you are using godly wisdom in the choices you are making?

THEN WHAT?
What commitment should you make in light of this passage?

EXTRA READING
JAMES 3

02.26.19 | TUESDAY
JAMES 4:13-17
DECISION MAKING

SAY WHAT?
Observation: What do I see?

SO WHAT?
Interpretation: What does it mean?

NOW WHAT?
Application: How does it apply to me?

THEN WHAT?
Implementation: What do I do?

Do verses 13-17 mean that we should not plan for the future? There are some who teach that these verses suggest just that. However, a closer examination of this section reveals a very different perspective. James' point is that there are many people who make plans for their future without ever considering God and what He might have planned for them. They have decided what to participate in in high school, what college to attend, where to work, any summer plans, etc., without ever considering what God would have them do. James is making the point here that we do not know what will happen tomorrow, so how can we make plans without considering God? Instead of making our own plans, we should seek His direction for our lives. Verse 17 takes it even a step further. To make plans without considering God is not only a bad idea, but it is sin. The one who knows that he ought to seek God's direction in making decisions and doesn't do it, sins. Not to seek what God wants you to do, in any decision you make, is to sin. What plans are you considering right now? Have you sought God's direction? Have you even considered what He might want you to do? If you have not, why not ask Him about it right now?

EXTRA READING
JAMES 4

ontrackdevotions.com

WEDNESDAY | 02.27.19
CREDIBILITY
JAMES 5:1-12

Do people consider you trustworthy? Do they always believe what you say without needing proof? Or, are you someone who has to prove or swear you are telling the truth? If you do not have credibility with people, you must have found verse 12 discouraging. James tells us that we should not be people who need to swear or prove that what we say is truth. Our character ought to be of such solid reputation that when we say yes, people know it means yes and, when we say no, people know it means no. Not to be known as someone who is honest and trustworthy is a serious blight for a Christian. Our truthfulness and character ought to be above reproach. If we give our word, it should be enough. People ought to know they can depend on us. If we make a commitment, they should know we will fulfill it. If we give our word, it means something. We need to strive to be the kind of people that James describes here. Our yes should always mean yes and, our no, no. How do you measure up to this standard? Do you have a reputation for being dependable? What will it take for you to become known as this kind of person? Use today's questions to help you get started.

SAY WHAT?
In what ways do people demonstrate that they are not someone who is trustworthy?

SO WHAT?
In what ways do you demonstrate that you are not a reliable person?

NOW WHAT?
How can you begin to improve in this area?

THEN WHAT?
In light of this passage, what personal commitment can you make?

EXTRA READING
JAMES 5

02.28.19 | THURSDAY

JAMES 5:13-20 — PRAYER

SAY WHAT?
Observation: What do I see?

SO WHAT?
Interpretation: What does it mean?

NOW WHAT?
Application: How does it apply to me?

THEN WHAT?
Implementation: What do I do?

Why did James use Elijah as the example of a righteous man who could do much through prayer? The reason should give you great hope. James tells us that the prayer of a righteous man is powerful and effective. Would the words powerful and effective describe your prayer life? It should encourage you to learn that all we have to do is be righteous, and we can have a prayer life that is powerful and effective. James uses Elijah as an example. In 1 Kings 18, we see Elijah is bold, courageous, confident, zealous, valiant, and empowered by God. All of these are characteristics we would expect from a righteous man. In chapter 19, we see that there were also occasions when Elijah was scared, discouraged, lonely, and blind to what God was doing. He doubted God's plan. You see, he was a man "just like us." Sometimes we are powerful and bold. Other times we are not. In reality, we are just like Elijah. James' point is that we, too, can be righteous and have a powerful and effective prayer life just like Elijah. What needs to change in your life to allow you to become a righteous man? Underline "just like us" to remind you it can be done.

EXTRA READING
JAMES 5

ontrackdevotions.com

WILDERNESS OUTFITTING

The longest-standing tool in our toolbox, the **Wilderness Outfitting** program presents an opportunity for the intentional leader to gain abnormal access to **real connection** with those they lead.

The wilderness can be leveraged into significant access to **real relationships** and **real conversations** that defy other environments... and it transfers back home beautifully.

LEARN MORE AT
SIMPLYAPILGRIM.COM/TRIPS

Photos by **Katie Hall** from a 2016 Pilgrimage trip with Ogletown Baptist Church (DE).
katiehallcreative.com

Be alert and of sober mind. Your enemy the devil prowls around like a roaring lion looking for someone to devour.

1 Peter 5:8 (NIV)

ontrackdevotions.com

 @ontrackdevos

 facebook.com/ontrackdevos

MARCH
2019
1 PETER - JUDE

MONTHLY PRAYER SHEET

"...The prayer of a righteous man is powerful and effective." James 5:16

Reach out...	How I will do it...	How it went...

Other requests...	Answered	How it was answered...

MONTHLY COMMITMENT SHEET

Name: _____

This sheet is designed to help you make personal commitments each month that will help you grow in your walk with God. Fill it out by determining
1. What will push you
2. What you think you can achieve

If you need help filling out your commitments, seek out someone you trust who can help you. Share your commitments with those who will help keep you accountable to your personal commitment.

Personal Devotions:
How did I do with my commitment last month? _____
I will commit to read the OnTrack Bible passage and devotional thought _____ day(s) each week this month.

Church Attendance:
How did I do last month with my attendance? _____
I will attend Youth/Growth Group _____ time(s) this month.
I will attend the Sunday AM service _____ time(s) this month.
I will attend the Sunday PM service _____ time(s) this month.
I will attend _____ time(s) this month.
I will attend _____ time(s) this month.

Scripture Memory:
How did I do with Scripture memory last month? _____
I will memorize _____ key verse(s) from the daily OnTrack Devotions this month.

Outreach:
How did I do last month with sharing Christ? _____
I will share Christ with _____ person/people this month.
I will serve my local church this month by _____

Other Activities:
List any other opportunities such as events, prayer group, etc., that you will participate in this month. _____

ontrackdevotions.com

FRIDAY | 03.01.19
REASONS FOR TRIALS
1 PETER 1:3-12

Why do trials come into the life of a believer? At times it almost seems as if the closer we move toward God, the more difficult the circumstances become in our lives. In today's reading, Peter reveals one reason why God allows trials to come into our lives. That reason should cause us to be encouraged and rejoice at the trials we face. In verse 7, we learn that sometimes trials come so we can see that our faith is genuine. Trials help us know for certain that we have eternal life and give us greater confidence that we have a personal relationship with God. It takes our faith from theory to reality. It makes our faith something alive in us that affects the way we live. And what happens when our faith becomes real? According to verse 7, it results in praise and honor when Jesus Christ is revealed. God uses trials to show us the reality of our faith. What are the trials in your life revealing? Do you know for certain that you have eternal life and are on your way to heaven? It may be that the trials you are now facing have been placed there by God to give you the opportunity to make your faith real. Trials are the means to a deeper, more personal relationship with Christ. Do you view trials this way?

SAY WHAT?
What trials are you facing right now?

SO WHAT?
How can you use these verses to help you face those trials and gain more authenticity in your walk with God?

NOW WHAT?
How can you use this passage to help someone you know who is going through a trial?

THEN WHAT?
In light of this passage, what personal commitment can you make?

EXTRA READING
1 PETER 1

03.02.19 | SATURDAY

1 PETER 1:13-21

EMPTINESS

SAY WHAT?
Observation: What do I see?

SO WHAT?
Interpretation: What does it mean?

NOW WHAT?
Application: How does it apply to me?

THEN WHAT?
Implementation: What do I do?

Have you ever read a passage of Scripture in which you saw something that stuck with you for a while? You kept thinking about it and could not get it out of your mind for several days. We find one of those phrases in today's reading. Did you notice it in verse 18? Peter described life before trusting Christ as being "empty." How true that is! Life without Jesus Christ is empty, even though it may be filled with friends and activities. We may achieve fame, or we may gain wealth, but it will all be empty. We may even gain power and freedom, but it will still leave us empty. Life with Christ, however, is fulfilling even though we may not have much of what the world deems valuable. We may not have material wealth and may not be well known, but we will still have a very full life. We may not have power, but we are content. When we trust Christ and He becomes real to us, our lives are full and exciting. With a lack of real commitment to Christ, any life we choose will leave us empty. Christ came to redeem us from "the empty way of life." If you claim to know Christ and claim He is real to you, yet your life is empty, something is wrong! That is not what Christ gave you. Who can help you figure out why?

EXTRA READING
1 PETER 1

ontrackdevotions.com

SUNDAY | 03.03.19

PROVERBS 28

The book of Proverbs was designed to help us in "attaining wisdom and discipline; in understanding words of insight; in acquiring a disciplined and prudent life, doing what is right and just and fair; in giving prudence to the simple, knowledge and discretion to the young." As you read through this chapter, write down the verses that are most significant to you in your present circumstances.

VERSE	WHAT TRUTH IT COMMUNICATES	HOW IT IMPACTS MY LIFE

03.04.19 | MONDAY

1 PETER 2:4-12

BUT NOW

SAY WHAT?
Observation: What do I see?

SO WHAT?
Interpretation: What does it mean?

NOW WHAT?
Application: How does it apply to me?

THEN WHAT?
Implementation: What do I do?

Did anything you read today in this passage make you think of yesterday's reading? Look at the words "but now" in verse 10. In today's reading, Peter talks more about our lives before we came to faith in Christ. Whom does he say we were before we trusted Christ? We were nobody. We had nothing and were nothing. But now, we are the people of God. We have gone from being nobodies to being children of the King. He also tells us that before Christ we were objects of God's wrath. We were sinners in need of forgiveness. But now, we have received mercy and our sins have been forgiven since we, by faith, trusted Christ. Therefore, according to verse 11, we should live as aliens in this world and abstain from sinful desires that war against us. We should live such good lives that even though the world accuses us of wrong doing, they still see our good deeds and glorify God. Our lives were empty because we were not the people of God and had not received mercy. But now our lives are full because we are the people of God and have found mercy through Jesus Christ. Circle the words "but now" to remind you of what Christ has done in your life. Live today as one who is forgiven

EXTRA READING
1 PETER 2

ontrackdevotions.com

TUESDAY | 03.05.19
UNJUST SUFFERING
1 PETER 2:18-25

How do you feel when you suffer for having done the right thing? Not only did you do nothing wrong, you actually did the right thing, but got punished anyway. Today's reading gives us practical principles regarding this kind of situation when it comes into our lives. Peter tells us that it is commendable to be someone who suffers for doing good. In fact, it might sober us to know that we should expect to suffer for doing good. Peter says it is something that we are "called" to do. Jesus Himself went through the same thing. He did so because He wanted to give us an example to follow. Christ is the ultimate example of one who suffered even though He did nothing wrong. How closely are you following His example? There was no deceit found in His mouth when he suffered. Is there any in yours? He hurled no insults to those who were mistreating Him. Do you? He did not retaliate when he was abused, but instead entrusted Himself to God the Father. Does this sound like you? What a powerful testimony this kind of life would be in our world today! What have you encountered that demands you follow the example of Christ? What needs to change for you to begin doing just that?

SAY WHAT?
In what situations are you finding it difficult to respond as Christ did?

SO WHAT?
How have you responded? Be specific.

NOW WHAT?
How can you use today's reading to help you respond like Christ when faced with unjust opposition?

THEN WHAT?
In light of this passage, what personal commitment can you make?

EXTRA READING
1 PETER 2

03.06.19 | WEDNESDAY
1 PETER 3:1-7 | SAME WAY

SAY WHAT?
Observation: What do I see?

SO WHAT?
Interpretation: What does it mean?

NOW WHAT?
Application: How does it apply to me?

THEN WHAT?
Implementation: What do I do?

What is Peter referring to in his admonition to wives and husbands when he says, "in the same way?" When we stop to think about it, we realize that this passage teaches that husbands and wives are to respond to their spouses in the same way that Christ responded in yesterday's reading. When circumstances are difficult and seem unfair in marriage, husbands and wives are not to react with insults, deception or retaliation. When one spouse is not being godly, the other party should not make any threats. Instead, he is to entrust himself to God. He alone is in control, and He alone has the solution. God tells us that He judges justly, and He will respond in due time. There is not a need to threaten, insult, or to retaliate. Jesus Christ is the example, and we are to respond in the same way as He did. If God allows you to enter into a marriage relationship, or if you're already married, you must be prepared to respond as Christ did, no matter what may take place. His example does not allow us the option of acting on our feelings. One way to prepare yourself, is to act in the same way in the relationships you have now. How are you doing in those areas? Responding "in the same way?"

EXTRA READING
1 PETER 3

ontrackdevotions.com

THURSDAY | 03.07.19
PROVIDING A REASON

1 PETER 3:8-17

Today, Peter continues the topic of how to respond to suffering that is undeserved. That is, being punished for something we did not do. In this passage, we are challenged in our responses to those who are evil toward us or insult us. Peter instructs us to continue to respond with kindness and goodness toward those who are in opposition to us. We must understand that we have been called to face this kind of suffering. In fact, in verse 14, Peter tells us that if we face this kind of opposition, we are blessed. He also tells us that our godly responses to this kind of suffering will often result in opportunities to share Christ with those who observe us. Peter tells us that we need to be prepared to share with people the reason why we are able to respond with kindness to those who are evil toward us. He tells us to not only be ready with the right message, but also be ready to share it with the right attitude--with gentleness and respect. We need to be able to respond to unjust suffering in the way Peter has described. And then, we should be able to provide an answer for our hope. Finally, we must be prepared to share the message with the right attitude. Are you? Do you know what to say with your next opportunity?

SAY WHAT?
What can you do to prepare yourself for unjust suffering?

SO WHAT?
What can you do to prepare yourself to give an answer to those who ask about your response?

NOW WHAT?
What can you do to prepare yourself to give the answer with the right attitude?

THEN WHAT?
In light of this passage, what personal commitment can you make?

EXTRA READING
1 PETER 3

03.08.19 | FRIDAY

1 PETER 4:7-11

MY ROLE

SAY WHAT?
Observation: What do I see?

SO WHAT?
Interpretation: What does it mean?

NOW WHAT?
Application: How does it apply to me?

THEN WHAT?
Implementation: What do I do?

In what ways has God gifted you to serve and encourage the body of Christ? If you can't answer that question, you can't fulfill what today's passage teaches. In verse 10, we're told to use whatever gift we have received to serve others. In other words, we are to take the gifts God has given us and invest them in the body of Christ. Think about the importance of this admonition in light of what we have been reading the past few days in 1 Peter. We have been told that as Christians, we are called to face all kinds of unjust suffering. While we know our suffering produces positive results in our lives, it is nonetheless difficult. It would be important to be a part of the lives of our brothers and sisters by using our gifts to serve and encourage them. Using our gifts might take different forms, but we must all use what we have been given. You can't afford to just sit back and not take your place. God has a purpose for your gifts. What do your gifts indicate to you about the role God might want you to play in your church? How can you use your gifts to serve the body of Christ? If you don't know what your gifts are, who can help you discover what they are and how you might use them to serve the body?

EXTRA READING
1 PETER 4

ontrackdevotions.com

SATURDAY | 03.09.19
SUFFERING
1 PETER 4:12-19

Before Peter closes this great book on suffering, he gives us a few final reminders. Did one of them stand out to you? Peter reminds us again that there are positive results from the suffering we face. He reminds us that we are able to participate in what Christ faced and that suffering allows us to bear His name. Insults resulting from our witness demonstrate that God's glory is upon us. We then have an opportunity to not only impact this world and grow in our walks with God through suffering, but also to affect our first meeting with Christ. Suffering allows us to have that first meeting with Christ be one of great joy. His final instructions on suffering? They are found in verse 19. Underline them in your Bible. First of all, we are to commit our lives to Christ and trust Him. Do not resist and worry, but give everything to Him. Secondly, continue to do good. Don't give in, don't stop doing what is right even in the midst of suffering. Allow God to use it in your life and in the lives of those who are watching. Why not take some time today to memorize this verse to help you handle any suffering you experience. Use today's questions to help you apply what you have been learning.

SAY WHAT?
Name one principle on suffering that you will take away from reading this book.

SO WHAT?
How can you apply it to your life right now?

NOW WHAT?
How can you better prepare yourself to respond correctly when suffering comes?

THEN WHAT?
In light of this passage, what personal commitment should you make?

EXTRA READING
1 PETER 4

PROVERBS 29

03.10.19 | SUNDAY

The book of Proverbs was designed to help us in "attaining wisdom and discipline; in understanding words of insight; in acquiring a disciplined and prudent life, doing what is right and just and fair; in giving prudence to the simple, knowledge and discretion to the young." As you read through this chapter, write down the verses that are most significant to you in your present circumstances.

VERSE | WHAT TRUTH IT COMMUNICATES | HOW IT IMPACTS MY LIFE

ontrackdevotions.com

MONDAY | 03.11.19
CLOTHED
1 PETER 5:5-7

What does it mean to be humble? How do we "clothe" ourselves with it in our relationships with each other? The word translated here humble or humility means lowliness of mind. It literally means the esteeming of ourselves as small. It means seeing ourselves as someone who is small and secondary to others. It is the opposite of pride, which is seeing ourselves as better than others. Being humble is not bragging or trying to put ourselves or our accomplishments forward. The word translated "clothe," in today's reading, means what you might imagine. To cling to something in the same way we put clothes on in the morning. Peter admonishes us to be humble people. We must view ourselves as small and not be prideful. We are then to get up each morning and "clothe" ourselves with this kind of an attitude throughout the day. We need to consciously remember what Christ has done for us and, not seek to exalt ourselves, but others. Clothing ourselves with humility means to intentionally think of ourselves as small and not the most important or the best person. Are you living successfully in this area? How can you improve being "clothed with humility?"

SAY WHAT?
Observation: What do I see?

SO WHAT?
Interpretation: What does it mean?

NOW WHAT?
Application: How does it apply to me?

THEN WHAT?
Implementation: What do I do?

EXTRA READING
1 PETER 5

03.12.19 | TUESDAY

2 PETER 1:3-11

EVERYTHING

SAY WHAT?
Observation: What do I see?

SO WHAT?
Interpretation: What does it mean?

NOW WHAT?
Application: How does it apply to me?

THEN WHAT?
Implementation: What do I do?

What is the difference between life and godliness in verse 3? Why does Peter distinguish between the two? The word translated "life" in this verse means life in the physical sense. It refers to our conduct or manner of living. It includes everything we do in the course of a regular day. The word for "godliness" is the spiritual aspect of one's life. It is a life that is acceptable to God. It is not inward holiness, but the outward manifestation of a walk with God. Peter is communicating that we have been given everything we need for the physical and spiritual areas of life. When someone becomes a Christian, he receives everything he needs to be effective in every area of his life, in both the spiritual and physical aspects. Some might think that the Bible, and our walks with God, involve only spiritual matters. That is not true!! Through salvation and God's Word, we have been given what we need both in the physical, day to day areas, and the spiritual areas of our lives. We possess everything we need to be good husbands and wives, good students or employees and good children and siblings. Are you accessing the Bible and the power of God in every area of your life? Why not begin using it today!

EXTRA READING
2 PETER 1

ontrackdevotions.com

WEDNESDAY | 03.13.19
MORE CERTAIN
2 PETER 1:16-21

How reliable is an eyewitness account? While it is most likely reliable, it is not 100% accurate. Why? Because even though we see something clearly, how we evaluate it or describe it can be influenced by many other factors. We may have been tired or upset. We each have our own opinions or biases that influence how we see something or interpret what we see. Knowing this makes the verses found in today's reading very important. Peter was an eyewitness to much of what is in Scripture, as were many of the authors. However, that is not why we can be sure that our Bibles are accurate. Peter tells us that the reason we can be sure that our Bibles are even more accurate than an eyewitness account is that they were not written according to the writers own interpretation. God is responsible for what was written in Scripture, and it is He who makes them accurate. Men recorded what they witnessed, but what they wrote was not their own opinions or interpretations of those events, but God's. You can have confidence that your Bible can be trusted and what you read is accurate. Additionally, beyond having confidence in it, according to verse 19, you will do well to pay attention to it!

SAY WHAT?
What outside factors might have influenced their descriptions of what they saw?

SO WHAT?
Why is this fact important to our understanding of Biblical inspiration?

NOW WHAT?
How can you use this passage to defend your view of Scripture with skeptics?

THEN WHAT?
In light of this passage, what personal commitment can you make?

EXTRA READING
2 PETER 1

03.14.19 | THURSDAY

2 PETER 2:1-10

HANG ON

SAY WHAT?
Observation: What do I see?

SO WHAT?
Interpretation: What does it mean?

NOW WHAT?
Application: How does it apply to me?

THEN WHAT?
Implementation: What do I do?

Have you ever been in the midst of a trial you thought would never end? Or, have you ever gotten to the point that you felt like giving up? Have you ever wondered if God was even aware of the circumstances that were going on in your life? If so, you will find encouragement in these verses. Peter reminds us that God knows how to rescue godly men from trials. Peter also lists for us a number of examples of how God responded to sinful people and held them accountable for the distress they inflicted on righteous people. He used the example of Lot. He lived in the midst of lawless circumstances and felt tormented for years. In time, God delivered him from it. Peter makes the point that God is able to deliver you as well. He stands to defend us against the sin of our world that seeks to inflict trials upon our lives. In the midst of incredible sin and hardship, God will deliver the godly while holding the unrighteous accountable. Are there circumstances in your life that require the hope this passage provides to keep you pressing forward? Is there someone who needs this hope? Why not share it with him? Never forget that God knows who you are, where you are, and He cares for you.

EXTRA READING
2 PETER 2

ontrackdevotions.com

FRIDAY | 03.15.19
FALSE TEACHERS
2 PETER 2:12-22

What can you learn about false teachers from this passage? One thing we can learn is that God has a very grim view of them. Another thing we see in these verses is the list of the characteristics for false teachers. Did you notice them? The first is that they take real Christian fellowship and distort it in order to practice their ungodliness. Opportunities that are meant to be good times of fellowship become times for false teachers to indulge their flesh. A second characteristic is that they use their positions and abilities to do spiritual work for personal gain. Their true motivation is to make money and not to help people. Although they had at one time displayed an appearance of godliness, the pattern of their lives illustrates that their true nature was far from God. We need to be careful in whom we place our trust and whose example we follow. In fact, we need to examine our teachers to make sure they are truly living according to God's standard. It is a blessing to have a teacher who is not like the men in this chapter. If your teacher is a godly man and not like the men in this passage, why not write and thank him. Let him know you are praying for him. It would be an encouragement to him.

SAY WHAT?
Observation: What do I see?

SO WHAT?
Interpretation: What does it mean?

NOW WHAT?
Application: How does it apply to me?

THEN WHAT?
Implementation: What do I do?

EXTRA READING
2 PETER 2

03.16.19 | SATURDAY
2 PETER 3:1-10
COMING SOON

SAY WHAT?
How can you be prepared for Christ's return?

SO WHAT?
In what specific ways can you tell if you really believe He will come back soon?

NOW WHAT?
How are you working to help others be prepared for Christ's return?

THEN WHAT?
In light of this passage, what personal commitment can you make?

Why hasn't Christ returned yet? When will He come again? To some, His delay indicates that He is not coming back at all. Peter closes this book by addressing the scoffers who claim that Christ is not coming back and lets us know why His return has been delayed. He first addresses the scoffers and speaks to some of their points. Some scoffers say that the evidence that Christ will not return is that things have gone on the same since the beginning of time. Peter reminds us that they have not taken into account that God had long ago judged the world by flooding the earth, which illustrates the absurdity of their point. Things have not continued the same since the beginning of time. Then, Peter explains that to God a day is like a thousand years. So to Him, it has only been about 2 days since He left the earth. Peter also explains that the return of Jesus Christ has been delayed to provide more people with the opportunity to be saved. His delay is not the neglect of His promise, but the fulfillment of it. When His patience has ended, He will come. The return of Christ has been delayed so that people you know will have an opportunity trust Christ. Will you be the one to tell them what Christ has done?

EXTRA READING
2 PETER 3

ontrackdevotions.com

SUNDAY | 03.17.19

PROVERBS 30

The book of Proverbs was designed to help us in "attaining wisdom and discipline; in understanding words of insight; in acquiring a disciplined and prudent life, doing what is right and just and fair; in giving prudence to the simple, knowledge and discretion to the young." As you read through this chapter, write down the verses that are most significant to you in your present circumstances.

VERSE	WHAT TRUTH IT COMMUNICATES	HOW IT IMPACTS MY LIFE

03.18.19 | MONDAY

2 PETER 3:11-18

GETTING IT WRONG

SAY WHAT?
Observation: What do I see?

SO WHAT?
Interpretation: What does it mean?

NOW WHAT?
Application: How does it apply to me?

THEN WHAT?
Implementation: What do I do?

Why do people have different interpretations of the Bible? One answer, though not a very comfortable one for us, is found in today's reading. Peter concludes this book with an admonition to live a godly life, and then encourages us in reading what Paul has written. Peter knows that some of what Paul wrote is not easy to understand. As a result, some people, who are ignorant and unstable, have distorted Paul's teachings and have led people astray with their wrong interpretations. We need to realize that sometimes people will share interpretations that are wrong, intentionally or unintentionally. They are wrong because those who make them are ignorant. They do not have the knowledge or skills they need to correctly handle the passage. It might also be wrong because they are unstable. They go back and forth between positions and beliefs. They are not firmly grounded in the Word. We need to be on our guard, lest we get carried away by false teaching. We need to make sure that our positions are based on solid interpretation principles and not just someone's ideas or opinions. It is too important to get it wrong!

EXTRA READING
2 PETER 3

ontrackdevotions.com

TUESDAY | 03.19.19
CHARACTERISTICS
1 JOHN 1:5-10

Today you begin a journey through the book of 1 John. This book contains important information about our salvation. It provides for us the characteristics of someone who is truly saved and the characteristics of someone who is not saved. It is a book that can give you assurance or reveal that you are not really saved. With this in mind, why not read through 1 John with that theme in mind, and record your discoveries. Each day, read the passage given and write down your observations in the space provided. Then, at the end of this book, examine your life to see if the fruits of true salvation are present. One important thing to keep in mind is that the Christian life is a process. While you may still struggle in areas that reflect the life of an unbeliever, they should be diminishing with time. You need to ask yourself if you see growth in those areas. You may not be happy with how much you have grown, but the question is are you making progress? Begin each day with prayer and ask God to reveal where you really stand before Him. You might want to involve others who will not only help you evaluate yourself, but help you do something about what you see.

SAY WHAT?
What characteristics of a believer does John reveal?

SO WHAT?
What characteristics of an unbeliever does John reveal?

NOW WHAT?
What do those characteristics reveal about your own salvation?

THEN WHAT?
In light of this passage, what personal commitment should you make?

EXTRA READING
1 JOHN 1

03.20.19 | WEDNESDAY

1 JOHN 2:1-11

OBEDIENCE

SAY WHAT?
What characteristics of a believer does John reveal?

SO WHAT?
What characteristics of an unbeliever does John reveal?

NOW WHAT?
What do those characteristics reveal about your own salvation?

THEN WHAT?
In light of this passage, what personal commitment should you make?

Continue the project we began yesterday. Read through today's passage and continue to write down the characteristics John lists for believers and unbelievers. Ask God daily to reveal the true condition of your heart through your discoveries from this book. Are you gaining assurance or becoming concerned with your findings?

EXTRA READING
1 JOHN 2

ontrackdevotions.com

THURSDAY | 03.21.19
LOVING THE WORLD

1 JOHN 2:12-17

Today we continue the project we began a couple days ago. Read through today's passage and continue to write down the characteristics John lists for believers and unbelievers. Remember to ask God daily to reveal the true condition of your heart through your discoveries from this book. Are you gaining assurance or becoming concerned with your findings?

SAY WHAT?
What characteristics of a believer does John reveal?

SO WHAT?
What characteristics of an unbeliever does John reveal?

NOW WHAT?
What do those characteristics reveal about your own salvation?

THEN WHAT?
In light of this passage, what personal commitment should you make?

EXTRA READING
1 JOHN 2

1 JOHN 3:1-10

03.22.19 | FRIDAY

CONTINUED SIN

SAY WHAT?
What characteristics of a believer does John reveal?

SO WHAT?
What characteristics of an unbeliever does John reveal?

We are on day 4 of the project we began in 1 John. Again today, read through this passage carefully and write down the characteristics you see that John gives for believers and unbelievers. Remember to ask God to reveal to you what your discoveries are telling you about your own spiritual condition. What have you been learning so far? Are you gaining assurance or becoming more concerned?

NOW WHAT?
What do those characteristics reveal about your own salvation?

THEN WHAT?
In light of this passage, what personal commitment should you make?

EXTRA READING
1 JOHN 3

ontrackdevotions.com

SATURDAY | 03.23.19
LOVE YOUR BROTHER
1 JOHN 3:11-24

We are on day 5 of the project we began in 1 John. Again today, read through this passage carefully and write down the characteristics you see that John gives for believers and unbelievers. Remember to ask God to reveal to you what your discoveries are telling you about your own spiritual condition. What have you been learning so far? Are you gaining assurance or becoming more concerned? Are you becoming concerned about someone else?

SAY WHAT?
What characteristics of a believer does John reveal?

SO WHAT?
What characteristics of an unbeliever does John reveal?

NOW WHAT?
What do those characteristics reveal about your own salvation?

THEN WHAT?
In light of this passage, what personal commitment should you make?

EXTRA READING
1 JOHN 3

03.24.19 | SUNDAY

PROVERBS 31

The book of Proverbs was designed to help us in "attaining wisdom and discipline; in understanding words of insight; in acquiring a disciplined and prudent life, doing what is right and just and fair; in giving prudence to the simple, knowledge and discretion to the young." As you read through this chapter, write down the verses that are most significant to you in your present circumstances.

VERSE | WHAT TRUTH IT COMMUNICATES | HOW IT IMPACTS MY LIFE

ontrackdevotions.com

MONDAY | 03.25.19

LOVE FOR OTHERS

1 JOHN 4:7-21

We are on day 6 of the project we began in 1 John. Again today, read through this passage carefully and write down the characteristics you see that John gives for believers and unbelievers. Remember to ask God to reveal to you what your discoveries are telling you about your own spiritual condition. What have you been learning so far? Are you gaining assurance or becoming more concerned?

SAY WHAT?
What characteristics of a believer does John reveal?

SO WHAT?
What characteristics of an unbeliever does John reveal?

NOW WHAT?
What do those characteristics reveal about your own salvation?

THEN WHAT?
In light of this passage, what personal commitment should you make?

EXTRA READING
1 JOHN 4

03.26.19 | TUESDAY

1 JOHN 5:1-12
LOVE FOR GOD

SAY WHAT?
What characteristics of a believer does John reveal?

SO WHAT?
What characteristics of an unbeliever does John reveal?

NOW WHAT?
What do those characteristics reveal about your own salvation?

THEN WHAT?
In light of this passage, what personal commitment should you make?

We are on day 7 of the project we began in 1 John. Again today, read through this passage carefully and write down the characteristics you see that John gives for believers and unbelievers. Ask God to reveal to you what your discoveries are telling you about your own spiritual condition. What have you been learning so far? Are you gaining assurance or becoming more concerned? Are you becoming concerned about someone else?

EXTRA READING
1 JOHN 5

ontrackdevotions.com

WEDNESDAY | 03.27.19
FINAL THOUGHTS
1 JOHN 5:13-21

This is the last day of the project we began in 1 John. Again today, read through this passage carefully and write down the characteristics you see that John gives for believers and unbelievers. Remember to ask God to reveal to you what your discoveries are telling you about your own spiritual condition. What have you been learning so far? Are you gaining assurance, or becoming more concerned?

SAY WHAT?
What characteristics of a believer does John reveal?

SO WHAT?
What characteristics of an unbeliever does John reveal?

NOW WHAT?
What do those characteristics reveal about your own salvation?

THEN WHAT?
In light of this passage, what personal commitment should you make?

EXTRA READING
1 JOHN 5

03.28.19 | THURSDAY
1 JOHN 5:13
THAT YOU MAY KNOW

SAY WHAT?
What characteristics did you see in your life that provide evidence of genuine salvation?

SO WHAT?
What characteristics did you see in yourself that are evidence of someone who is not saved? Have you observed any growth in these areas?

NOW WHAT?
Summarize what these answers tell you about where you stand in your relationship to God.

THEN WHAT?
In light of the conclusions you have come to, what do you need to do now? How are you going to do it?

We have just completed reading through this great book and jotting down our observations of the characteristics of believers and unbelievers. John closed this book with the statement "I write these things to you... that you may know that you have eternal life." As you read through it, did you see evidence of your salvation? What conclusions have you come to about your own walk with God? Has your reading given you assurance? Has it revealed that you have eternal life, but you need some work in specific areas? Or, has it revealed that you do not truly have eternal life? Use today's questions to help summarize what you have learned. Be honest about what you have found. Then talk to someone who can help you understand what it means, as well as how to respond in a Biblical manner. Remember to be a doer of the Word, not just a hearer! Has it caused you to become concerned about the spiritual condition of someone else? What can you do to be helpful to them?

EXTRA READING
MISSED PASSAGES

ontrackdevotions.com

FRIDAY | 03.29.19
WALK IN TRUTH
2 JOHN 1-6

What does it mean to "walk in the truth?" Knowing people were "walking in truth" brought John great joy. How do we know if we are walking in the truth? Walking in the truth simply means that you have ordered your life according to the Word of God. It means you know what the Bible says, and you are obeying it in every area of your life. In fact, according to verse 6, our love for Christ is demonstrated by our obedience to His commands. To disobey what the Bible says is to show that we do not truly love Christ. Additionally, walking in the truth means that people who observe us see an individual who is honest. Walking in the truth means we do not gossip or make fun of others. Walking in the truth means that we are obedient to our parents and show them respect, even when they are not around to hear what we are saying. Walking in the truth means that our speech always reflects Christ. You see, walking in the truth means that our lives and conduct are consistent with what the Bible teaches. Could it be said of you that you "walk in the truth?" Are there areas of your life in which you do not? Does your walk bring joy to those who teach you? What needs to change?

SAY WHAT?
Observation: What do I see?

SO WHAT?
Interpretation: What does it mean?

NOW WHAT?
Application: How does it apply to me?

THEN WHAT?
Implementation: What do I do?

EXTRA READING
2 JOHN

03.30.19 | SATURDAY

3 JOHN 9-15

IMITATION

SAY WHAT?
In what ways are you like Diotrephes?

SO WHAT?
In what ways are you unlike Diotrephes?

NOW WHAT?
What characteristics do you need to change in order to be less like him and more like Christ?

THEN WHAT?
In light of this passage, what personal commitment can you make?

Who do people say you remind them of? The answer to that question could reveal a lot to you about yourself. John shares in this short book that we are to imitate what is good. That is, we ought to remind people of good things and good people. We should not be imitating people or things that are wrong. John uses Diotrephes as an example of imitating what is wrong. He was someone who obviously imitated evil. John tells us that he was a man who loved to be first. He must have been very selfish for others to have observed this in him. Would people in your world describe you this way? John also wrote that he was someone who maliciously gossiped about others. What conclusions would we come to if we listened to what you talked about today? To make matters worse, Diotrephes refused to welcome other brothers. Do you? When a new person comes to your school or church, do you reach out to him and make him feel more comfortable? Diotrephes wouldn't have. Does any of this sound like you at all? What kind of reputation do you have? Do your friends and acquaintances think of you like John did of this man? What needs to change or improve in what or whom you imitate?

EXTRA READING
3 JOHN

ontrackdevotions.com

SUNDAY | 03.31.19
PRAYING
JUDE 17-25

What does it mean to pray in the Spirit? How does one do that? There is often confusion about what Jude is asking us to do in this passage, but the answer is really quite simple. To pray in the Spirit means to be guided and led by Him. It means that we are not led by our own selfishness when we pray. That would not be praying in the Spirit, but praying in the flesh. We also pray in the flesh when we pray using our own intellect. We request what seems to make sense to us and do not pray according to God's wisdom. Praying in the flesh also might include asking God to energize what we want instead of seeking His will and desires. Praying in the Spirit is not a mystical thing that only spiritual people can do. It is something we all can and should do. How do we accomplish this? By letting God control our wants, and seeking His will rather than our fleshly desires. Examine your prayer life. Are you praying in the flesh or in the Spirit? Is it God's will you are seeking or your own? Are you selfishly asking God to conform to what you want or are you asking Him to conform you to what He desires? What needs to change in order for you to pray in the Spirit?

SAY WHAT?
How can you determine if you pray in the flesh?

Look at how selfish my prayers are.

SO WHAT?
In what ways do you see evidence that you are praying in the Spirit?

NOW WHAT?
What can you do to begin to eliminate your flesh from dominating your prayer life?

THEN WHAT?
In light of this passage, what personal commitment should you make?

EXTRA READING
JUDE

PILGRIMAGE

WILDERNESS INSTITUTE
FOR LEADERSHIP DEVELOPMENT

"One of the most effective tools for change I have ever seen... the perfect environment for God to work, resulting in permanent life change."

COLLEGE AND GRADUATE COURSE CREDIT AVAILABLE THROUGH OUR PARTNERSHIPS WITH:

LEARN MORE AT
SIMPLYAPILGRIM.COM/WILD

Breathe PARTNERS

SCHOOL of MINISTRY

"I have been given countless opportunities to put action to the things I believe and this frontline experience has changed my ministry forever. The School of Ministry has increased my determination to learn and has grown my faith to lead."

ACCREDITED DEGREE PROGRAMS AVAILABLE THROUGH OUR PARTNERSHIP WITH

ANCHOR
CHRISTIAN UNIVERSITY

LEARN MORE AT
BREATHEPARTNERS.COM/SOM

THE LAUNCH INITIATIVE

STRONG BIBLICAL FOUNDATION

INTENSIVE SPIRITUAL FORMATION

MINISTRY EXPERIENCE & PREPAREDNESS

CUSTOMIZED TRAJECTORY

Arrowhead's Gap Year Program - The Launch Initiative (TLI) is an intensive discipleship and leadership training program designed to give graduated high school students real life experience prior to further education, finding a career or starting a family. TLI is a "Bridge" that provides crucial mentoring, living skills training, personal development and healthy community in the unique camping ministry context of Arrowhead Bible Camp. TLI uses a missions support platform, challenging students to develop a missional mindset, create a network of ministry supporters and experience lifestyle ministry with the opportunity to complete the program debt free.

The Launch Initiatve is a two semester experience with our Shepherds Camp summer programming as a prerequisite. Students will live onsite at Arrowhead during the summer and for two semesters which correspond to the fall and winter retreat seasons. Each semester will include a combination of experience-based academics, spiritual formation & growth, professional training and ministry experience.

PURSUING GOD WITH PURPOSE
PREPARE - PERFORM - PRODUCE

SHEPHERDS CAMP
Arrowhead's unique program for adults with developmental disabilities. Transforming the way you love and care for others.

GUEST GROUPS
We provide the incredible experience of camp. Learning to serve with excellence and create dynamic ministry partnerships.

JAMES PROJECT
High impact missions on the front lines at Arrowhead. Creating the next level of ministry partnership that changes lives & trains leaders.

TRAINING LEADERS
Arrowhead is a high intensity, experience-based training ground for our staff & students. Pursuing God - engaged in ministry and taking the next step.

www.abclaunch.org

Here I am! I stand at the door and knock. If anyone hears my voice and opens the door, I will come in and eat with them, and they with me.

Revelation 19:6 (ESV)

ontrackdevotions.com

 @ontrackdevos

 facebook.com/ontrackdevos

APRIL
2019
REVELATION

MONTHLY PRAYER SHEET

"...The prayer of a righteous man is powerful and effective." James 5:16

Reach out...	How I will do it...	How it went...

Other requests...	Answered	How it was answered...

MONTHLY COMMITMENT SHEET

Name: _____

This sheet is designed to help you make personal commitments each month that will help you grow in your walk with God. Fill it out by determining
1. What will push you
2. What you think you can achieve

If you need help filling out your commitments, seek out someone you trust who can help you. Share your commitments with those who will help keep you accountable to your personal commitment.

Personal Devotions:
How did I do with my commitment last month? _____
I will commit to read the OnTrack Bible passage and devotional thought _____ day(s) each week this month.

Church Attendance:
How did I do last month with my attendance? _____
I will attend Youth/Growth Group _____ time(s) this month.
I will attend the Sunday AM service _____ time(s) this month.
I will attend the Sunday PM service _____ time(s) this month.
I will attend _____ time(s) this month.
I will attend _____ time(s) this month.

Scripture Memory:
How did I do with Scripture memory last month? _____
I will memorize _____ key verse(s) from the daily OnTrack Devotions this month.

Outreach:
How did I do last month with sharing Christ? _____
I will share Christ with _____ person/people this month.
I will serve my local church this month by _____

Other Activities:
List any other opportunities such as events, prayer group, etc., that you will participate in this month. _____

ontrackdevotions.com

MONDAY | 04.01.19

A BLESSING

REVELATION 1:1-11

Today you begin a journey that might be brand new for you, but one that should inspire you--a journey through the book of Revelation. It is a book that everyone seems to be interested in, but one that few have read through completely. As you start, keep in mind significant points John opens with in this first chapter. The first point is that this book is the revelation of Jesus Christ that God gave to John. It is not John's opinion or his perception. What you will be reading came to John from God, and he simply wrote down what he had seen(vs11). Second, it is important to know the reason God gave John this book. God wanted you to be able to know what will soon take place(vs1). It is your preview of the future. Third, this book comes with a promise from God that you will be blessed if you read it, hear it, and take to heart its message. Although you may not catch everything the first time through, you will learn much that will challenge you. Ask God for insight as you begin. Use today's questions to help you get started.

SAY WHAT?
What do you hope to gain from reading this book?

SO WHAT?
What do you hope to learn?

NOW WHAT?
What will you need to do in order to see these two goals take place?

THEN WHAT?
In light of this passage, what personal commitment should you make?

EXTRA READING
REVELATION 1

04.02.19 | TUESDAY

REVELATION 2:1-7 — FIRST LOVE

SAY WHAT?
How can you tell if you or your church has lost its first love?

SO WHAT?
How can you remember, repent and return to your first love?

NOW WHAT?
How can you avoid losing your first love in the future?

THEN WHAT?
In light of this passage, what personal commitment can you make?

Over the next seven days, we will be reading God's messages to the seven churches. These were actual churches at the time this book was written. In most cases, the letters contain positive characteristics along with some negative issues. Today, we read about the church in Ephesus. This was a church that had much to be proud of. God said they had persevered in the midst of hardship due to their testimony for Christ. It was not a church that had given in when the heat was turned up. It was also a church that did not tolerate wickedness. But, in spite of all those positives, they had lost their first love. The joy and excitement they once had in their faith was gone. The fire that had once burned bright was out, and they were just going through the motions. God called on them to remember where they had been in their relationship to Christ. They were also told to repent for falling away and return to their first love. Have you or your church lost the fire and passion you once had for Christ? If so, remember, repent, and do what you once did. Losing your first love has serious consequences. Do not let it happen to you.

EXTRA READING
REVELATION 2

ontrackdevotions.com

WEDNESDAY | 04.03.19
HANDLING OPPOSITION
REVELATION 2:8-11

What would you do if you heard that some students from your school or your fellow co-workers were going to rough you up because of your stand for Christ? What if you were told they would be waiting for you after school or work? That is exactly what had happened to the church in Smyrna. This church had two characteristics written about it. It had afflictions and it was poor. Yet, in the midst of all that, God saw that they were rich. They did not allow their afflictions or poverty to cause bitterness or discouragement to develop. God told them not to be afraid of what they were about to endure. God informed them that Satan would attack them. Some would be put into prison and suffer for ten days. Their challenge? To remain faithful so that God could give them the crown of life. It must have given them great comfort to realize that God knew exactly what was going on in their lives. He would help and then reward them for their faithfulness. Are you experiencing opposition in which you need to be faithful and maintain your stand? Just like the church of Smyrna, God knows what is going on in your life and will respond. Underline verse 10 to remind you to remain faithful.

SAY WHAT?
What opposition do you face or might you face at school or work if you take a stand?

SO WHAT?
What could God desire to accomplish in your life through it?

NOW WHAT?
How can today's reading help you be faithful in the midst of opposition?

THEN WHAT?
In light of this passage, what personal commitment can you make?

EXTRA READING
REVELATION 2

04.04.19 | THURSDAY

REVELATION 2:12-17

DOCTRINE

SAY WHAT?
Observation: What do I see?

SO WHAT?
Interpretation: What does it mean?

NOW WHAT?
Application: How does it apply to me?

THEN WHAT?
Implementation: What do I do?

How important is it to keep wrong doctrines out of the local church? According to today's reading, it is crucial. God tells the church in Pergamum that He was pleased with areas of their church. Amazingly, they remained true to God's name even when one of their leaders had been put to death. They did not renounce their faith, but stood firm in what they believed. There was, however, a problem. There were some in the church of Pergamum who were in error doctrinally. One such group was the Nicolaitans. They taught that Christians had total liberty after salvation. According to them, this freedom included free love. Premarital and extramarital sex was permitted. Although this church had not denounced Christ, purity of doctrine was not a priority to them. If allowed to continue, this teaching would have caused many to fall into great sin and would have eventually led some to denounce Christ. While some would argue that doctrine is not important as long as you love God, this passage clearly indicates otherwise. We need to make understanding the truth of the Scriptures our priority.

EXTRA READING
REVELATION 2

ontrackdevotions.com

FRIDAY | 04.05.19
FALSE TEACHING
REVELATION 2:18-29

Was there an actual woman named Jezebel in the church at Thyatira? Possibly, but it probably referred to a well known woman in the church whose actions resembled those of Jezebel in the Old Testament. How does this impact what God is saying in this section? God informed this church that He saw they were a people who loved and served others. They also demonstrated faith and perseverance. In fact, God saw that they had improved in these areas and were even more successful than they had been at first. But, in the same way as the church at Pergamum, they tolerated a woman who called herself a prophetess and taught Scriptural error. She misled the believers in this church, teaching that sexual immorality was acceptable. Some believe she was possibly teaching that homosexuality and premarital sex were permissible--as long as those involved professed love. God's judgment was imminent. He would not tolerate this in the church. We, likewise, must never allow any teachings that contradict what the Bible says. Would you be able to identify false teaching if you heard it? Another reason to stay faithful to your daily Bible reading!

SAY WHAT?
Observation: What do I see?

SO WHAT?
Interpretation: What does it mean?

NOW WHAT?
Application: How does it apply to me?

THEN WHAT?
Implementation: What do I do?

EXTRA READING
REVELATION 2

04.06.19 | SATURDAY

REVELATION 3:1-6
SPIRITUALLY DEAD

SAY WHAT?
What signs of spiritual life and power do you see in your church?

SO WHAT?
What evidence is there in your church or your life to indicate that you are close to dying?

NOW WHAT?
What needs to happen to change that condition?

THEN WHAT?
In light of this passage, what personal commitment can you make?

What does the definition of the word "dead" include? The answer is important for all of us. Can you imagine being in the church at Sardis when this letter was read? They must have all sat quietly waiting to hear what God would say about them. He began the letter by saying that He knew their deeds and was aware of their reputation of being alive. These believers were known for their spiritual enthusiasm and power. They must have been pleased with what they heard, but the statement that followed was shocking. Their reputation for enthusiasm was well known, but God knew that they were really spiritually dead. Characteristics attributed to their church were not actually true. There was no spiritual life or power. His challenge was to wake up. He warned them that the "life" that remained was about to die. How those words must have stung. To regain their "life," they must remember, obey, and repent. Could this be said about your life or your church? Do people think you are alive, but inside you know you are dead? If so, you need to heed the word yourself to "remember, obey, and repent!" Today can be the day it all changes!

EXTRA READING
REVELATION 3

ontrackdevotions.com

SUNDAY | 04.07.19

PROVERBS 1

The book of Proverbs was designed to help us in "attaining wisdom and discipline; in understanding words of insight; in acquiring a disciplined and prudent life, doing what is right and just and fair; in giving prudence to the simple, knowledge and discretion to the young." As you read through this chapter, write down the verses that are most significant to you in your present circumstances.

VERSE	WHAT TRUTH IT COMMUNICATES	HOW IT IMPACTS MY LIFE

REVELATION 3:7-13

04.08.19 | MONDAY
ONLY POSITIVE

SAY WHAT?
Observation: What do I see?

SO WHAT?
Interpretation: What does it mean?

NOW WHAT?
Application: How does it apply to me?

THEN WHAT?
Implementation: What do I do?

What is the difference between this letter and the other letters we have read so far? One obvious difference is that there wasn't one negative statement about this church. Can you imagine what emotions these believers felt when this letter was read? What joy they must have felt to hear that God was pleased with their lives and that He would give them an open door that no one could shut. Their ministry was guaranteed to be successful! Although their strength was small, they had remained true to His name and His Word. They also learned that those who opposed and criticized them would one day admit that God did love them. They were comforted by the knowledge that God would keep them from the hour of trial--to take them away so they wouldn't have to face it. How would God evaluate you and your church? It should encourage us all to realize that it is possible for God's evaluation of a church to be positive. Could He describe your church in this same way? What needs to change for this to be true? What contribution can you make to change things so that God could say only positive things about your church?

EXTRA READING
REVELATION 3

ontrackdevotions.com

TUESDAY | 04.09.19
AVERAGE
REVELATION 3:14-22

On a scale of 1-10, how would you rate your spiritual life? Choose a number before you read on further. How do you think God feels about where you are spiritually? If you gave yourself a number in the middle, these verses should bother you. Many people evaluate their spiritual lives and willingly admit that they are not where they should be. They find comfort in the misguided thought that God is pleased with the lack of blatant sin in their lives. In this letter, God clearly states that average or lukewarm Christianity is worse to Him than being a cold Christian. How do you think the Laodiceans felt when they realized what God's position on average was? Why is lukewarm so sickening to God? According to verse 17, it is because it leads us to a wrong conclusion about our level of spiritual maturity. A lukewarm individual can convince himself that he is doing fine and needs nothing. In reality, to God he is poor, wretched, pitiful, blind, and naked. God's counsel to lukewarm Christians is to repent and come back to Him. How does God feel about your spiritual life? Does it make God sick? Do you need to repent and come back?

SAY WHAT?
How did you rate your spiritual life on the scale of 1-10 and why did you give yourself that number?

SO WHAT?
How does God feel about where you are in your walk with Him?

NOW WHAT?
What needs to change in order for you to move to a higher number?

THEN WHAT?
In light of this passage, what personal commitment should you make?

EXTRA READING
REVELATION 3

 #ontrackdevos

04.10.19 | WEDNESDAY
REVELATION 4:5-11 — WORTHY

SAY WHAT?
Observation: What do I see?

SO WHAT?
Interpretation: What does it mean?

NOW WHAT?
Application: How does it apply to me?

THEN WHAT?
Implementation: What do I do?

If someone were to ask you who Jesus Christ is, how would you describe Him? Often, someone who was saved as a small child does not fully grasp who Jesus is and what He has done for him. It is easy to focus on the attributes of Christ and forget what He has done in our lives. In this chapter, we see how an understanding of what Christ has done impacts our view of Him. To the four creatures, Christ is holy. Their focus is on His attributes, and they are awed by who He is. To the 24 elders, Jesus Christ is worthy. Why? Because they had been redeemed by Christ, their focus is not only on who He is, but also on what He did for them personally. He is not only an all-powerful and all-knowing God, but He humbled Himself and died on the cross for their sins. Jesus Christ changed their lives forever. Creatures who cannot experience redemption will never know what it is like to see Jesus as worthy. Do you fully understand who Jesus is and what He has done for you? Does your heart overflow with gratitude when you consider what Christ has done in your life? Have you told Him? Take time today to reflect not only on who Christ is, but also on what He has done for you.

EXTRA READING
REVELATION 4

ontrackdevotions.com

THURSDAY | 04.11.19
READY?

REVELATION 5:9-14

Have you ever thought about what the events mentioned in this chapter will be like? Should you and I expect to be a part of them? The events written about in the following chapters will all take place during the Tribulation Period. The rapture will have previously taken place, and those of us who have trusted Christ as Savior will be in heaven. The events that will take place on the earth during this time period will not be something we will experience. We will already be in heaven and will only participate in the events that occur there. We will join the heavenly host and those redeemed throughout the ages singing "Worthy Is the Lamb." It will be a wondrous choir with all of us able to harmonize perfectly. What an awesome moment! On earth, however, those who do not know Christ will be facing the judgment and wrath of God. While we are singing and praising God, times of great peril are about to begin on the earth. Where will your friends and family be during the Tribulation? Are they ready? Have you told them what the Bible says about their future? When will you?

SAY WHAT?
Observation: What do I see?

SO WHAT?
Interpretation: What does it mean?

NOW WHAT?
Application: How does it apply to me?

THEN WHAT?
Implementation: What do I do?

EXTRA READING
REVELATION 5

REVELATION 6:1-8

04.12.19 | FRIDAY

SEAL JUDGMENTS

SAY WHAT?
Of all the judgments listed in this passage, which one do you think will be the worst?

SO WHAT?
Why do you think Christians are so passive about wanting to keep unsaved people from these judgments?

NOW WHAT?
What can you do to allow these truths to impact the way you live?

THEN WHAT?
In light of this passage, what personal commitment should you make?

Today, we begin reading the record of what will take place on the earth while those of us who have trusted Christ will be in heaven. We will be in heaven awaiting the end of the Tribulation and our return with Christ for the 1,000 year rule on the earth. The first judgments to take place are the seven seal judgments. Six of the seven are found in today's extra reading. The first seal judgment is the beginning of a cold war on the earth. Distrust and suspicion will rule. The second seal judgment is open war. Bloodshed will be the norm. The third seal judgment is famine. According to the Bible, the famine will be so severe that a day's wages will buy only one quart of wheat. The fourth seal judgment is death. One fourth of the world's population will die. The fifth seal judgment is martyrdom. Christians will be slain for their faith in Christ. The sixth seal is physical disturbances. Meteor showers, earthquakes, and other examples are given. People on earth will know that God's wrath has begun. How thankful we should be that we will be in heaven. It should also motivate us to share Christ with others so they can avoid God's judgment.

EXTRA READING
REVELATION 6

ontrackdevotions.com

SATURDAY | 04.13.19

SALVATION CONTINUES

REVELATION 7:1-8

Why did God pause between His description of the sixth and seventh seal judgments to explain the 144,000 sealed Jews? It would be easy for one to read this chapter and conclude that no one could possibly get saved in the midst of all the horror occurring on the earth. It is as though God stops the account to let us know that, in spite of what is transpiring on the earth, He will continue to save people. The activity of grace and opportunities to trust in the Son of God for salvation will continue. John tells us that 144,000 Jews will be saved as well as "a great multitude that no one could count." This group will be made up of all kinds of people. What a comfort to know that no matter how awful the circumstances may seem to us or, how wicked this world may yet get, God is still willing to reach out and save people. In spite of the circumstances, people will see their need to trust Christ. That alone ought to encourage us to continue sharing our faith, regardless of the circumstances. Don't assume that you will get a negative response when looking for opportunities to share Christ with your world. Use today's questions to help you get started.

SAY WHAT?
List the names of some people in your world who you would like to see come to Christ?

SO WHAT?
What obstacles could keep you from sharing Christ with them?

NOW WHAT?
How are you going to share Christ with them?

THEN WHAT?
In light of this passage, what personal commitment can you make?

EXTRA READING
REVELATION 7

 #ontrackdevos

04.14.19 | SUNDAY

PROVERBS 2

The book of Proverbs was designed to help us in "attaining wisdom and discipline; in understanding words of insight; in acquiring a disciplined and prudent life, doing what is right and just and fair; in giving prudence to the simple, knowledge and discretion to the young." As you read through this chapter, write down the verses that are most significant to you in your present circumstances.

VERSE | WHAT TRUTH IT COMMUNICATES | HOW IT IMPACTS MY LIFE

ontrackdevotions.com

MONDAY | 04.15.19
SILENCE
REVELATION 8:1-5

Why was there silence in heaven after the seventh seal was opened? As we read this chapter, we realize silence is about the only response one could have to what will be taking place. While the seal judgments are horrible, these next judgments are even worse. Can you imagine what it is going to be like to live on the earth during the Tribulation? Think about it! In the trumpet judgments, a third of the earth will be burned up, a third of the sea will be turned into blood and, as a result, a third of the creatures in the sea will die. Imagine the smell from all the death and decay. Judgment continues with a third of the rivers becoming bitter, and even more people will die. Then, a third of all light from the sun and moon will be removed, which means a third of each day will be totally black. How horrible it will be to live on the earth during this time period. How does the knowledge of this affect you? You need to be more diligent in sharing the message of Christ with those who are headed for these judgments because they are not saved. Take advantage of the opportunities that God gives you this week to share the message of hope.

SAY WHAT?
Observation: What do I see?

SO WHAT?
Interpretation: What does it mean?

NOW WHAT?
Application: How does it apply to me?

THEN WHAT?
Implementation: What do I do?

EXTRA READING
REVELATION 8

04.16.19 | TUESDAY

REVELATION 9:1-11

IN CONTROL

SAY WHAT?
Observation: What do I see?

SO WHAT?
Interpretation: What does it mean?

NOW WHAT?
Application: How does it apply to me?

THEN WHAT?
Implementation: What do I do?

Who controls the demonic forces that come out of the abyss for the fifth trumpet judgment? It may seem, as you read this, that the events unfolding during the Tribulation reveal that things are out of control. It would appear that God has lost His hold on the situation. I am sure it will also appear that way to the people on earth during these events. However, that is not the case. According to verses 4-5, the demons can do only what God will allow them to do. Their activities and their power will be limited by God. All the events of the Tribulation are still under God's control. As we continue our reading throughout this month, we must keep this critical truth in mind. Difficult circumstances cloud our ability to see reality. When evil appears to be winning and God seems to be losing, we often feel that the situation is out of control. In His sovereign judgment, God may allow difficult circumstances to take place, but He is always directing them. Have you recently felt as though God has lost control in your life? Keep in mind our view of a situation is limited. God is still in control.

EXTRA READING
REVELATION 9

ontrackdevotions.com

WEDNESDAY | 04.17.19
OUR RESPONSE
REVELATION 10:8-11

Why did God ask John to eat the scroll? Is there a message for us in this event? In this chapter, John saw a book that contained more of the events that were yet to come. John was told not to reveal them. Then, he was asked to do something that must have seemed really strange. He was told to take the scroll and eat it. He was told that it would taste sweet in his mouth, but would then grow sour in his stomach. Why? Could God be showing that before we can communicate His Word, it must be inside of us? Could He also be demonstrating the truth of this entire book? Prophecy is exciting to read and study. However, when we really look at it and think about it, it sours in our stomachs. This book, while exciting and interesting, ought to grieve the heart of every believer. What happened to John when he ate the scroll should happen to each of us. What does your response to this book tell you about your concern for the lost? Are you burdened to reach people who will experience these events? "The harvest is plentiful but the workers are few" (Matthew 9:37). Will you be one of the few?

SAY WHAT?
What are some of the most interesting facts you have learned so far this month in Revelation?

SO WHAT?
What is the most difficult truth to accept?

NOW WHAT?
What should your response be to what you are learning?

THEN WHAT?
In light of this passage, what personal commitment can you make?

EXTRA READING
REVELATION 10

04.18.19 | THURSDAY

REVELATION 11:1-14

PUNISHMENT

SAY WHAT?
Observation: What do I see?

SO WHAT?
Interpretation: What does it mean?

NOW WHAT?
Application: How does it apply to me?

THEN WHAT?
Implementation: What do I do?

How do you respond to the judgment of God in your life? When punishment comes as a result of your sin, how well do you receive it? Hopefully, it is not like the people in today's reading. Today we read about the two witnesses who will be on the earth at this time. Even after experiencing all that has taken place to this point, the world will not respond well to their message. For 1,260 days, the witnesses will preach, and people will not be able to harm them, although they will try. The witnesses will then be killed. The world will respond by celebrating their deaths. Not only will they refuse to properly bury them, but the two witnesses will be left in the street for all to see. The world will then use the occasion as a holiday in which they send one another gifts. Amazing! But God will again intervene by raising the two witnesses from the dead and taking them to heaven. He also will send an earthquake as judgment. What is the message for us today? It is so important that we not allow the judgments of God to harden us, but soften us and bring us to repentance. When punishment comes, we need to submit to it and let it teach us (Heb. 12:11).

EXTRA READING
REVELATION 11

ontrackdevotions.com

FRIDAY | 04.19.19

SATAN'S PLAN

REVELATION 12:1-9

After reading this passage, do you understand what it means? It is not an easy passage to comprehend. But to help us, we need to closely examine what John has written. First, the woman in this chapter refers to the nation of Israel. It is from the Jews that Christ was born. The child is obviously Christ. The dragon is Satan. Satan had tried, at the time of Christ's birth, to destroy Him. He was unable to, and Christ fulfilled the purpose for which He was sent. He died for our sins and rose again on the third day, overcoming sin and death. Since Satan was unable to defeat the child, he turned his attention to the woman, Israel. We also learn that there will be a battle between the forces of the Archangel Michael and those of Satan. Satan will be defeated and then cast out of heaven. He will no longer be permitted in heaven. Satan will respond by intensifying his attack on Israel. However, God will provide refuge so that they will not be defeated. What we read about here is the beginning of the end for Satan and his army. God will be victorious, and He will provide deliverance for His people. He always does!

SAY WHAT?
Observation: What do I see?

SO WHAT?
Interpretation: What does it mean?

NOW WHAT?
Application: How does it apply to me?

THEN WHAT?
Implementation: What do I do?

EXTRA READING
REVELATION 12

04.20.19 | SATURDAY
REVELATION 13:1-12 — HOPELESS?

SAY WHAT?
What circumstances are you now facing that seem to be hopeless?

SO WHAT?
What situation can you look back on to confirm that God provided a way through it for you?

NOW WHAT?
How can you find comfort from this passage in your present circumstances?

THEN WHAT?
In light of this passage, what personal commitment can you make?

Who is the first beast in this chapter, and who is the second beast? The first beast is commonly known as Antichrist. He is a man who will rule on the earth during the tribulation and will be given his power and his throne by Satan himself. The second beast is known as the false prophet. His job will be to promote the Antichrist and convince the world to worship him. Satan is attempting to counterfeit the trinity of God with these two evil beasts. He will set himself up as God and the Antichrist as Jesus. Satan will even deceive people into believing that the Antichrist has died of a head wound and is then raised back to life. All this is designed to counterfeit what God has done. It would seem hopeless if we did not know that God was in total control. While Satan may think he is in control, he is just accomplishing what God has designed. The saints are given great encouragement in verse 10 when they are told to have patient endurance and faithfulness. Likewise, when we face what may appear to be hopeless situations, we need faithfulness and endurance as we wait for God's solution. God is in control even when it may look like He is not.

EXTRA READING
REVELATION 13

ontrackdevotions.com

SUNDAY | 04.21.19

PROVERBS 3

The book of Proverbs was designed to help us in "attaining wisdom and discipline; in understanding words of insight; in acquiring a disciplined and prudent life, doing what is right and just and fair; in giving prudence to the simple, knowledge and discretion to the young." As you read through this chapter, write down the verses that are most significant to you in your present circumstances.

VERSE	WHAT TRUTH IT COMMUNICATES	HOW IT IMPACTS MY LIFE

REVELATION 14:1-13

04.22.19 | MONDAY
BLAMELESS

SAY WHAT?
Observation: What do I see?

SO WHAT?
Interpretation: What does it mean?

NOW WHAT?
Application: How does it apply to me?

THEN WHAT?
Implementation: What do I do?

How much does our environment impact how we behave? If we live in the midst of wickedness and rebellion, does that mean we must cave in to peer pressure? If you feel as if there is no hope for people who live in very difficult situations, then this passage should encourage you. We read today about the 144,000 who had been saved and go to heaven. Their work on earth was completed. In spite of all that had happened on the earth, they remained pure. They did not defile themselves with women. This could simply mean that they were unmarried or refer to the fact that they were sexually pure. They followed the Lamb even though the world around them did not. That is a true definition of standing alone in the midst of great opposition. Their world was filled with lies and deceit, yet they did not lie. In fact, according to verse 5, they were blameless. What an encouragement that should be to us. It illustrates that we, too, can remain blameless with God's power even in the midst of great wickedness. We can stay pure in the midst of sexual immorality. In the midst of rebellion, we can stand firm. Are you standing firm? You can!

EXTRA READING
REVELATION 14

ontrackdevotions.com

TUESDAY | 04.23.19
STILL STANDING   REVELATION 15:1-4

Chapter 15 is an interlude before the most awesome of God's judgments against the world begins. In chapter 16, we will begin learning about the seven bowl judgments, which are even worse than what we have read so far. As we discover what will be taking place in heaven, there is something important to keep in mind. Did you notice it? It is found in verse 2. As John looked across the sea, he saw a group of people. Note how he described them. They were a group who had been victorious over the beast. It would be logical to feel that Satan would control everyone during the Tribulation. However, there still will be people who will not succumb to his deception, and will remain faithful to God. In fact, some will even trust Christ, as we read earlier. As we continue our reading and learn about the bowl judgments ahead, keep in mind that there will still be those who stand firm for God and resist Satan and his schemes. How much more, in this present day and age, should we stand against Satan and live victoriously for Christ? What is keeping you from taking a stand in your world?

SAY WHAT?
Observation: What do I see?

SO WHAT?
Interpretation: What does it mean?

NOW WHAT?
Application: How does it apply to me?

THEN WHAT?
Implementation: What do I do?

EXTRA READING
REVELATION 15

04.24.19 | WEDNESDAY
REVELATION 16:1-11 | HARD HEARTS

SAY WHAT?
How does God reveal areas to you in which you need to repent?

SO WHAT?
In what areas do you see Him prompting you right now?

NOW WHAT?
How can you avoid developing a hard heart that refuses to repent?

THEN WHAT?
In light of this passage, what personal commitment should you make?

Why would a God of love bring about these horrible judgments on the earth? We are given part of the answer in this chapter. As you read these verses, you can't help but shudder at what it is going to be like on the earth during the bowl judgments, especially when you realize what has already taken place. Everyone will have painful sores all over their bodies. Every living thing in the sea will die, and the rivers and springs will become blood. Imagine the agony and outcry when people are not just sunburned, but are scorched and seared. Why? According to verse 6, they had shed the blood of saints and prophets. They, even in the midst of all these judgments, will refuse to humble themselves before God and repent or respond meekly to the people who serve Him. Even verse 9 says that, in spite of their own physical pain from the sores and the sun, they will refuse to acknowledge their sin or glorify God. How does this end? With an earthquake unlike any before. Their response? No repentance. Sin left not dealt with can lead to unbelievable hardness. Make sure you deal with sin immediately so you won't become hardened!

EXTRA READING
REVELATION 16

ontrackdevotions.com

THURSDAY | 04.25.19
FALSE RELIGIONS
REVELATION 17:1-8

This is one of the chapters in Revelation that can be very confusing. It helps us to understand the passage by understanding some of the symbols given here. The beast, of course, as we learned earlier, is the Antichrist. The harlot is the false religion that has been the world's religion during the Tribulation. John explains that, during the beginning of the Tribulation, this false religion will flourish in the system of the world referred to as Babylon. This false religion will be centered in Rome, and will be comprised of many religious groups including the Roman Catholic Church. For the first half of the Tribulation, this religion will reign unchallenged. In the middle of the Tribulation, however, the Antichrist will destroy this religion and will set himself up as the one to be worshiped. John describes what this religion will look like. He also tells us that all the world will follow it until it is destroyed by the Antichrist. In spite of what has gone on to this point, people will still refuse to acknowledge God, and continue to worship the beast. In spite of all that has happened, people will not repent. Unfortunately, we can be just like them. Are you?

SAY WHAT?
Observation: What do I see?

SO WHAT?
Interpretation: What does it mean?

NOW WHAT?
Application: How does it apply to me?

THEN WHAT?
Implementation: What do I do?

EXTRA READING
REVELATION 17

04.26.19 | FRIDAY

REVELATION 18:9-20

JUDGMENT COMING

SAY WHAT?
What gives people confidence in a successful future?

SO WHAT?
What is going on in our world that causes people to wonder if God is going to win?

NOW WHAT?
How can you apply today's reading to both situations?

THEN WHAT?
In light of this passage, what personal commitment should you make?

Today you have read the final aspect of the judgment of God on the world. In it, we find some important and interesting facts. Chapter 17 revealed how the religion of Babylon will end. Chapter 18 reveals how the economic and commercial aspects of Babylon will end. Not only will Babylon become the center for the religion of the world during the Tribulation, it will also become the commercial center of the world. In spite of all that has happened on the earth so far, Babylon will still give people hope because of its wealth and power. Just read verses 11-13 and see the kind of luxury items that will still be sold out from this city. When God comes to destroy it, people will finally grasp the fact that it is all about to end. As they see this city burning from the judgment of God, they will realize that this great city and its wealth and power is about to fall under the mighty hand of God. How can you apply this passage to your own life? Although it may appear that God is not going to win and all looks hopeless in your world, He will always be victorious. He will always judge sin and He will always deliver the righteous. Have hope!

EXTRA READING
REVELATION 18

ontrackdevotions.com

SATURDAY | 04.27.19
VICTORY
REVELATION 19:11-21

What a difference between this chapter and the other chapters we have been reading so far this month! Instead of gloom and doom, today we see the beginning of God's reign on the earth. As you read these events, remember that, if you know Christ as your Savior, you will be participating in them. After the destruction of Babylon we read about yesterday, Christ will come back to earth to set up His earthly kingdom. Heaven will begin rejoicing knowing that the time has almost arrived. Christ will mount His white horse and come to earth to destroy Satan and his armies. The beast and false prophet will be captured and cast into the lake of fire. Imagine the armies of the earth gathering for one final battle and the excitement they'll feel as they all unite against God and His army. With such great might, they are confident and certain that God will be defeated. How that will all change when the beast and the false prophet are captured! All this was designed to prepare the earth for God's rule. God's kingdom will be ready to begin its rule. That will be an awesome day! Will you be one of those who will enter it? Who in your world will not?

SAY WHAT?
Observation: What do I see?

SO WHAT?
Interpretation: What does it mean?

NOW WHAT?
Application: How does it apply to me?

THEN WHAT?
Implementation: What do I do?

EXTRA READING
REVELATION 19

04.28.19 | SUNDAY

REVELATION 20:1-6

TRUE SALVATION

SAY WHAT?
When did you, by faith, trust Christ as your Savior? Why did you trust Him?

SO WHAT?
What evidence do you see in your life that you have been truly saved?

NOW WHAT?
How can you tell if your actions are the result of your salvation and not just outward conformity to Christianity?

THEN WHAT?
In light of this passage, what personal commitment can you make?

Who are the rest of the dead referred to in verse 5? Where do the people who side with Satan at the end of the 1,000 years come from? The answer is found in the passage. There are two resurrections mentioned in Scripture. The first is of those who have died and have been saved. Those who died without Christ will not be resurrected at this time. John is referring to these unsaved people in verse 5. Only those who are saved will enter into the 1,000 year reign of Christ. Christians who are alive on the earth at the end of the Tribulation will also enter into the 1,000 year reign with their human bodies. These are the people who will continue having children throughout the 1,000 years. Although everyone will have to be obedient to Christ and His rule during this time, there will be some who will not turn to Christ for salvation. This proves that living in a perfect world and doing all the right things outwardly are not enough to make you a child of God. Man's heart changes only when he turns to Christ for salvation. No amount of outward effort or conformity will do. Following the culture, even the "Christian culture," is not enough.

EXTRA READING
REVELATION 20

ontrackdevotions.com

MONDAY | 04.29.19
HEAVEN
REVELATION 21:1-14

These last two chapters of Revelation address what it will be like in eternity for those of us who have accepted Christ as our Savior. Chapter 21 deals with the city of Jerusalem, and chapter 22 shows the blessing for us who will be living on the new earth forever. It is truly overwhelming when we comprehend all the wonderful things God has prepared for us who have trusted Christ. What makes this city even greater is not the material that is used, not the construction, not its size, but who will be there. It is a city in which God will dwell. There will be no need for light because His glory will shine and, no need for a temple, for He will be present to worship. Think about what it will be like to live there with your saved loved ones and friends, all the saints of the Bible and, especially, Jesus Christ. It is heartbreaking to realize there are those who will not be going to live in glory. If it is you, allow both the horrors of God's judgment and the glory of our eternal home to motivate you to trust Christ. If it is someone you know, let it motivate you to share Christ with the ones you care about who are unsaved. You can't sit by and let them miss out!

SAY WHAT?
Observation: What do I see?

SO WHAT?
Interpretation: What does it mean?

NOW WHAT?
Application: How does it apply to me?

THEN WHAT?
Implementation: What do I do?

EXTRA READING
REVELATION 21

04.30.19 | TUESDAY

REVELATION 22:12-21

THE END

SAY WHAT?
What impressions have you had as you read this book?

SO WHAT?
How do you hope to be different because of what you have read?

NOW WHAT?
How are you going to implement those changes?

THEN WHAT?
In light of this passage, what personal commitment should you make?

Your journey is over. You have just completed reading the book of Revelation. Hopefully, you leave it with a greater understanding of the end times. In the very first chapter, we read that blessings await those who read, hear, and take to heart the words of this book. As you have read of both the horrible events and the wonderful events that are ahead, you have rejoiced in knowing that you are not going to experience the horrible things that will take place in the future. Hopefully you have been motivated to serve God more faithfully and have gained a greater burden to reach out to those in your world with what Christ has done for them. They may then avoid the Tribulation and an eternity without Christ. Our time is slipping away, and Jesus Christ will return soon. Make sure you and the unsaved people you know are ready. Take some time today to reflect on what God has confronted you with as you have read Revelation this month. Don't walk away from it unchanged! Use today's questions to jot down some ways you want to change. Remember, God's blessing awaits those who read it and take to heart what is written!

EXTRA READING
REVELATION 22

ontrackdevotions.com

Made in the USA
Middletown, DE
07 January 2019